A SHORT HISTORY

of the

WORLD *in*

50 LIES

Also in the series:

A Short History of the World in 50 Places
A Short History of the World in 50 Animals
A Short History of the World in 50 Books

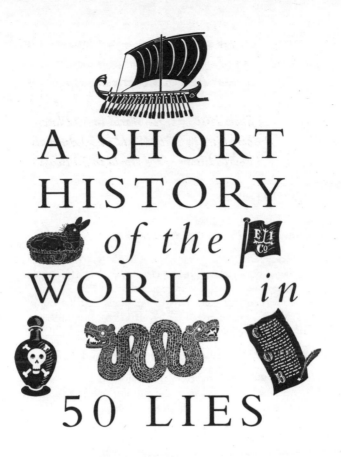

A SHORT HISTORY *of the* WORLD *in* 50 LIES

Natasha Tidd

Illustrated by Emily Feaver

Michael O'Mara Books Limited

To Martyn Tidd, my dad, my friend, and favourite reader.
Thank you. We started this together and finished apart.
Words aren't enough, but here are some.

First published in Great Britain in 2023 by
Michael O'Mara Books Limited
9 Lion Yard
Tremadoc Road
London SW4 7NQ

A CIP catalogue record for this book is available from the British Library.

This product is made of material from well-managed, FSC®-certified forests and other controlled sources. The manufacturing processes conform to the environmental regulations of the country of origin.

ISBN: 978-1-78929-460-6 in hardback print format
ISBN: 978-1-78929-526-9 in trade paperback format
ISBN: 978-1-78929-462-0 in ebook format

2 3 4 5 6 7 8 9 10

Designed and typeset by Claire Cater
Printed and bound by CPI Group (UK) Ltd, Croydon, CR0 4YY
www.mombooks.com

MIX
Paper | Supporting
responsible forestry
FSC
www.fsc.org   FSC® C171272

CONTENTS

Part III: The Early Modern Age

Part IV: The Nineteenth Century

INTRODUCTION

If you're anything like me, then when you were growing up, your parents taught you not to lie. This is a fairly universal lesson – lying is bad. That's not to say we don't lie; indeed, multiple studies have found that lying is an inherent part of human nature, and who hasn't told a white lie to protect feelings or get out of a spot of trouble? Still, we continue to tell our children not to lie, and for good reason. Even when we put aside morals and ethics and just focus on the practicality of the thing, lying is more often than not a damaging practice that tends to spiral out of control, creating chasms and domino effects that are impossible to reverse. If this is the effect that lying can have on our individual lives, then you can imagine the immense impact it's had on history.

The history of lies is irrevocably devastating, encompassing the rise and fall of ideologies, religions and empires. This book contains just fifty of those lies, some linked across the centuries, others appearing self-contained, but each falsehood ripples down the timeline. We'll explore the evolution of lying, beginning in the Ancient World with the early days of the art of political spin and cover-ups. Moving on to the Middle Ages, we start to be presented with a trend of rewriting history to fit a present narrative, alongside the use of literature in pushing forward false agendas and ideology. Once we reach the Early Modern Age, we'll see how these basic elements of lying start to snowball beyond control, combining with the growth of conspiracy theories and widespread forgeries. With the new technology of the nineteenth century comes the rise and development of fake news – from funny hoaxes to catastrophically world-changing pieces of journalism. Finally, in the twentieth century, we'll witness the culmination of the lie's evolution, including a mass cover-up of colonial atrocities to propaganda wars, and a piece of fake news that helped kill millions.

Over the next fifty chapters, we'll traverse some of the darkest events in human history. At times it can feel inescapably bleak, but in that mire of lies there is always light. Because, when we peel back the lies of history, we can gain a better understanding of not only history itself but the legacies of the past we're left with today. This isn't so much a book about uncovering the truth, as it is one of untangling the web of deceit that hid it and looking at why that web was there in the first place.

Part I

THE ANCIENT WORLD

THE FAKE BARDIYA

In ancient history, one of the most cited and lauded figures is Darius the Great, the third Achaemenid King of Kings. Under his rule the Achaemenid Persian Empire would stretch beyond its Iranian roots, its tendrils encompassing West Asia, the Caucasus, the Balkans and parts of Central Asia and Egypt. His work in consolidating the power and wealth of the empire, maintaining religious tolerance, and interconnecting the lands he'd won has marked him as one of the few rulers who truly earned the moniker 'great' that was bestowed on them. Yet this story contains one very big lie. Darius was not the third King of Kings – he was the fourth. And how he bumped off that forgotten ruler, erasing their rights from historic memory, tells us a great deal about who Darius really was.

Beginning its formation in 550 BC, the Achaemenid Persian

Empire was built from the success of Cyrus the Great, who in the space of his almost thirty-year reign between 559 and 530 BC managed to conquer the Medes, Lydia and the Neo-Babylonian Empire. To carry on the fledgling empire's march to power, Cyrus had two heirs to pick from, his sons Cambyses and Bardiya. Of the two, Bardiya was arguably the more capable at governance, with Cambyses known for being highly unstable, yet Cambyses was the elder of the two and so when Cyrus died in 530 BC, it was Cambyses who came to power, crowned Cambyses II. To begin with, things went smoothly, and although Cambyses exhibited something of a despotic tendency, the early years of his reign were pretty uneventful. This would change when he began to prepare to invade Egypt. Cambyses claimed to have had a series of prophetical dreams, in which Bardiya had snatched control of his empire. Rather than dismissing these as just dreams or investigating their validity, Cambyses threw any sense of caution to the wind and ordered the secret assassination of his brother and cover-up of his death. With the murder done, Cambyses appeared to regain focus and went on to conquer Egypt.

But killing your brother tends to come with consequences. For Cambyses, this was that when he died, in July 522 BC, there was no direct heir to take his place. With the role of ruler up for grabs, a very unusual frontrunner appeared – Bardiya. Of course, this wasn't the real Bardiya, but a fake in the form of a magus called Gaumāta, who in early 522 BC had begun impersonating him. While Cambyses was in Egypt, this fake Bardiya was back in Persia rallying support against his 'brother', leading to a short-lived rebellion that was quelled when Cambyses died and the usurper Bardiya was crowned King of Kings. For those who had been close to Cambyses II, this was an injustice that could not stand – they knew that the real Bardiya had been secretly killed and so this new king had no right to rule and could jeopardize the entire empire. In September 522 BC, Cambyses's lance bearer, Darius, led a group of men to entrap and murder Gaumāta. With the false king dead, Darius had saved the Achaemenid Empire and was duly crowned its new ruler, Darius the Great.

This is Darius's account of events, which can be found inscribed in the Behistun Inscription, a huge testimony of his rise to power carved into Mount Behistun in western Iran, that he had inscribed sometime between 522 and 486 BC. However, curiously for such a historic coup, there are only two major sources of evidence to back up Darius's claims – the Behistun Inscription and the Greek historian Herodotus, who included the tale of the fake Bardiya in his 430 BC tome, *Histories*. Much of Herodotus's retelling comes directly from the Behistun Inscription, with the rest being fictional flourishes that have no historical grounding. In Herodotus's version, Gaumāta is replaced by two brothers named Patizeithes and Smerdis. Patizeithes is a kind of puppet master who lies his way into making Smerdis king. Their ruse is only foiled when it is discovered that, unlike the real Bardiya, Smerdis does not have ears.

LYING TO LEGEND

The Behistun Inscription is accompanied by a vast carving, which shows Darius the Great looking up at the symbol of Faravahar, signifying his divinity and right. Crushed into the dirt underneath Darius's foot is a figure assumed to be Gaumāta, showing that no usurper can take away a true king's rule.

Herodotus's inclusion of the brothers and the subsequent ear-based investigation makes his version a little too far-fetched to be truly believed. However, Darius the Great's account is by no means without its own glaring flaws. Historians have pored over these gaping holes in logic – if Cambyses did indeed secretly kill his brother in 525 BC, how did nobody notice Bardiya's absence, and how did Gaumāta know of the death in order to be able to successfully impersonate Bardiya? To kill an imperial prince at the time would have been near impossible to cover up. With the Egyptian campaign looming, members of the royal family were bound to participate, which would mean that Bardiya's absence would have been noted and recorded. The only reason that he wouldn't have participated would be if he was working as regent elsewhere, in which case, again, his sudden disappearance would appear in records. Similarly, if Bardiya had indeed been secretly killed and then suddenly re-emerged three years later in the guise of Gaumāta this would have made it to historical records. Bardiya was the son of Cyrus and brother of Cambyses, so he was a well-known figure whose movements would have been tracked.

So, what actually happened to Bardiya? The likely answer is surprisingly simple. There was no fake Bardiya. Bardiya wasn't killed in 525 BC but was in Persia acting as regent ruler while his brother was fighting in Egypt. From Babylonian documents, we can see that in 522 BC Bardiya appears to have started a campaign against his brother, being named '*King of Babylon, King of Lands*' in the spring of that year, several months before Cambyses's death and Bardiya's official accession. As to why Darius the Great fabricated the story of the fake Bardiya, it's another simple answer – to gain power. Much like Cambyses, Bardiya had no heirs, so if he died, the rule of the Achaemenid Empire would be up in the air. Darius almost certainly took advantage of this situation, killing Bardiya and creating the myth of the fake Bardiya to cement himself as the saviour of the empire and secure his place at the head of it.

Despite his likely duplicitous route to the top, Darius the Great became known as one of the greatest rulers of the Achaemenid Empire, reigning over it at its territorial and cultural height. However, this wouldn't last for long. Darius's heir and successor, Xerxes, was not quite as skilled in the art of lying as his father, a characteristic that would ultimately help lead to the downfall of an empire.

THEMISTOCLES AND THE MESSAGE TO XERXES

When Xerxes I came to power following the death of his father, Darius the Great, in 486 BC, the Achaemenid Persian Empire was at its peak. However, with such a huge land mass, rebellions were frequent. As soon as he took the throne Xerxes was headed to Egypt to quell a revolt, which was quickly followed by two more uprisings in Babylonia in 484 BC. Xerxes's successes in managing these situations cemented him as not only a capable – if sometimes ruthless – ruler, but one with military might behind him. So, it's unsurprising that only a few years into his reign, Xerxes decided to do something his father had long dreamed of but had never been able to achieve – Xerxes was going to conquer Greece.

Invading Greece was no easy task. Darius the Great's first invasion, in 492 BC, ended with a crushing defeat within only two years. Hoping to avoid making the same mistakes,

Xerxes heavily invested in not only his military forces but building bridges and waterways that would allow his soldiers and ships to better pass into Greece. By 481 BC, Xerxes was finally ready and troops from across the Achaemenid Persian Empire gathered for the invasion. In response, the Grecian States formed a united front against the invading Persians, led by forces from Athens and Sparta. But Xerxes's preparation had proved itself a winning formula and by 480 BC, his forces were steadily working their way beyond the Greek coast. City after city folded in the wake of the greatest army Greece had yet encountered, and in late summer the two sides would meet in their first major battle, at Thermopylae. Seven thousand Greek soldiers, with three hundred Spartans at their heart, formed a barrier through the narrow pass – they were vastly outnumbered, but the land they'd entrenched themselves in wouldn't allow for Xerxes to unleash his full force. For two days the sides hacked away at each other, each force Xerxes sent into the pass coming back in defeat. Finally, Xerxes moved his troops to outflank the Greeks. As they moved in, much of the Greek force abandoned the fight, leaving behind the remaining Spartans and several hundred men from the Thespiae division to undertake a suicide mission in holding back the Persian forces as long as possible.

After Thermopylae, Xerxes seemed unstoppable. His forces quickly captured more land and burned cities that resisted, as a warning to others. By the late summer of 480 BC, Athens was captured and Xerxes ordered its immediate destruction. He was now well on his way to seizing much of mainland Greece, but to secure his path to victory, Xerxes still needed to defeat the

Greek navy, which was now sitting off the coast of the island of Salamis, directly opposite the coast of Athens, separated only by the Saronic Gulf. Once more the Greek forces were outnumbered and another decisive victory for Xerxes looked imminent. However, Greece had an ace up its sleeve, Athenian general and politician Themistocles.

THIS IS SPARTA!

The battle at Thermopylae birthed the myth of the 300, helped in no small way by Herodotus lionizing the Spartan leader, Leonidas, and his men, as brave fighting machines standing firm for immortal glory. This in turn cemented the popular myth that in battle all Spartan troops would either win or choose to fight to the death.

While most of the Greek leaders were pressing to abandon their position in Salamis – after all, defeat was inevitable – Themistocles was fighting to stay. The waters off Salamis were narrow and he believed that the ships could use this to their advantage, utilizing their smaller fleet to entrap Xerxes's mammoth ships in the Salamis straits. This was a risky strategy, as a similar tactic had been used at Thermopylae, resulting in defeat. However, Themistocles knew something else. Xerxes had eyes and ears within the Greek camp and would by now have heard that the Greeks were fighting over what to do at Salamis, and so Themistocles laid a trap.

An envoy was sent with a message for Xerxes – Themistocles and his Athenian forces had been betrayed by the other Greek contingents and they now wanted to side with Xerxes. To cement Xerxes's belief in this lie, Themistocles added that Xerxes should strike now, while the other Greek ships were preparing to flee, and the Athenian force was ready to help him fight. Xerxes fell for it hook, line and sinker.

The Persian ships entered the Salamis straits, and at first it seemed Themistocles had been true to his word. As they advanced, several of the Greek ships looked to be attempting to flee – but this was just a ploy to lure Xerxes's forces further into the narrow waters. The Greeks surrounded the Persian ships and attacked. It was a brutal defeat and proved a turning point in Xerxes's grand invasion plans. With much of his naval fleet destroyed, Xerxes opted to retreat, taking most of the army back to his empire and leaving a small contingent to continue the battle with Greece – this group was defeated in 879 BC.

As if losing to a far smaller force wasn't embarrassing enough for Xerxes, in the wake of Greece's victory it began to take back Achaemenid-owned Greek territories. Around 466 BC, Xerxes made another attempt to gain a foothold in Greece, but this too proved to be a failure. Xerxes had begun his reign as a strong military ruler, but by his final years his missteps were showing the weaknesses of the Achaemenid Empire and this would prove fatal. In 465 BC, Xerxes was assassinated in a mysterious plot – ironically much like that of Darius the Great's – to seize the throne. The Achaemenid Empire would never again be as powerful as it was in Xerxes's heyday and would ultimately fall in 330 BC to the armies of Alexander the Great.

Julius Caesar and the Invention of Spin

In the centuries following the fall of the Achaemenid Persian Empire, another great global superpower was rising up – the Roman Republic – and in 58 BC one of its most historically known characters was poised to mastermind a very modern innovation – political spin.

Prior to becoming known as one of the empire's greatest statesmen, and well before the Ides of March, Julius Caesar was a man drowning in a seemingly endless sea of debt – in 61 BC alone, he had taken out an unprecedented large loan from one of the Republic's richest men, Crassus, yet already in debt, he had no means to pay off such a monstrous bill. Climbing the ladder of political power in the Roman Republic was an expensive game, each rung costing a fortune, and if those bribes and creditors were not paid off, a politician wouldn't just become bankrupt but face a formal ban from political life. This was the fate that awaited Julius Caesar. He'd just finished his tenure as 59 BC consul, the highest magisterial role possible, and had been awarded a five-year pro-consulship, which included operations over two Roman-run areas of Gaul – yet if he didn't fix his debt problem, and fast, he would lose everything.

But Caesar thought that in Gaul he might just have found his get-out-of-jail-free card. Gaul itself was a mammoth swathe of Western Europe, encompassing modern-day France, Luxembourg, Belgium, and parts of Germany, Switzerland, Italy and the Netherlands. Most of Gaul was independent, run by nations and tribes; however, Caesar hoped to change this. If he could start a war with part of Gaul, it could help him get out of debt. Gaul was full of riches waiting to be plundered, and Rome's bustling slave trade was always looking for prisoners of war to snap up. All Caesar needed to do was find a reason to strike, and a confederation of Gallic tribes named the Helvetii looked to be about to provide him with just that.

The Helvetii occupied much of Gaul's Swiss Plateau and in 58 BC they asked Caesar for permission to pass through his Roman-run lands so they could migrate to the west. Caesar refused, hoping the Helvetii would break into his lands, giving him the go-ahead for battle. But the Helvetii took the peaceful approach, opting to find another route. Not about to let his meal ticket escape, Caesar gathered his legions and followed, ambushing the migrating mass as they tried to cross the River Saône. The fight that followed almost wholly massacred the Helvetii's Tigurini tribe. Several bloody skirmishes followed until the Helvetii were defeated and returned to their land to act as a buffer between Rome and the more hostile parts of Gaul, particularly the dangerous Germanic tribes. A now substantially richer Caesar had found a winning formula – go to war, get out of debt, gain power. And so began the Gallic Wars.

Yet, Caesar's plan had one big flaw. To keep climbing the ranks of the Roman Republic, he needed to maintain his image, and going to war as a debt crisis measure wasn't exactly a good look. He had to offer the Republic a different rendition of the truth, one that made his actions seem beneficial, not just for him, but for all Romans. So Caesar decided to publish his own version of events in a series of ongoing reports, *Commentarii de Bello Gallico* (*Commentaries on the Gallic War*). Here, Caesar explained that he had to pursue the Helvetii as they were planning to migrate next to a Roman Province and as such were a dangerous threat to all Romans (the Helvetii were in fact migrating 320 km (200 miles) away from this area). As for the massacre of the Tigurini tribe, Caesar claimed this as divine intervention, the Tigurini having played a small part in the death of one of Caesar's wife's ancestors fifty years earlier in 107 BC. This account is perhaps the most notable early example of political spin, bending the truth to justify the means.

Throughout the Gallic Wars, Caesar utilized his new-found propaganda machine to transform wartime atrocities into just and rightful moves. The 57 BC sale of 53,000 members of the Belgian-based Nervii nation into slavery is blamed not on greed, but enemy conspiracy and oath-breaking. The sacking of the villages of the Eburones tribes in 53 BC is cited as a necessary measure so Caesar could capture a rebel leader, and when he couldn't find said rebel, he had *no* choice but to burn down the Eburones' homes and crops in 51 BC, forcing them into starvation. Stating that while they were alive, they would *'never allow him to return'*. Perhaps the most outlandish piece of spin comes from Caesar's 55 BC massacre of civilians from the Germanic Usipetes and Tencteri nations, claiming that most were not killed by Caesar's forces but tragically committed mass suicide after losing *'any hope they were getting away'*.

GETTING THE GAUL

The Gallic Wars would be crucial in terms of Caesar's rise to becoming dictator of Rome. When the war came to a close in 50 BC, Caesar had conquered all of Gaul and part of Britain, becoming wealthy beyond any previously conceived probability and kicking off what would become almost five centuries' worth of Roman rule over Gaul.

Interestingly, Caesar's spin was taken as fact, not just by the Roman Republic and later the Roman Empire, but by history. Indeed, *Commentaries on the Gallic War* was actually celebrated as one of the greatest war reports of all time until the mid-twentieth century. What eventually tipped historians off to Caesar's lies wasn't his dubious justifications, but his use of numbers. In *Commentaries* Caesar claims to have conquered huge armies; for example, he declared that the Usipetes and Tencteri had been 430,000 strong and that in their defeat, no Roman soldier had died. Unlikely Roman fatalities aside, when comparing Caesar's statistics to those found in modern research of the era, it became apparent that the Usipetes and Tencteri having a force of that size was an impossibility for the time and Caesar had inflated the magnitude of his enemy in a calculated effort to boost his reputation. This investigation of military figures opened the floodgates, and soon every aspect of Caesar's claims was under historical investigation.

It took over two thousand years for Julius Caesar's clever web of lies to be untangled and today *Commentaries on the Gallic War* is seen not as a piece of historic fact, but as one of the earliest examples of political spin and the dangers that come with it.

CICERO'S *PHILIPPICS*

Caesar's pioneering of the art of spin didn't end with him. In fact, his assassination would open the door for another Roman statesman, Marcus Tullius Cicero, to take Caesar's methods one step further, blurring the lines between propaganda and spin to birth one of the earliest incidences of fake news.

On 15 March 44 BC, Julius Caesar had just been named *'dictator for life'* and was enjoying the heady heights of his tyrannical rule of the Roman Republic, when he was surrounded by a group of rival senators. Each held a knife and, believing that no man should wield absolute power and if one person had to wield such power, it should definitely *not* be Caesar, they unleashed a volley of death blows. These men saw themselves as liberators, saving the people from a despot. However, the people themselves didn't feel the same. Caesar had been incredibly popular with the lower and middle classes and they saw his death as a desperate power grab by the one per cent. Infighting and anarchy broke out and in the midst of this was Marcus Tullius Cicero. He had not been involved in the plot to kill Caesar but was overjoyed to hear of the dictator's death. Cicero hoped that he could seize upon this as an opportunity to turn the tide and return the Republic to the political state it had been in before Caesar's rule. Yet to do this, he'd need to align himself with Caesar's successor.

There were two parties vying for the job, Caesar's right-hand man, Mark Antony, and Caesar's great-nephew and adopted son, Octavian. Caesar had actually named Octavian as his successor in his will; however, the boy was just eighteen and relatively inexperienced. In comparison, Mark Antony had gained mass support following Caesar's death and was seen as the de facto heir and leader of the Caesarian faction. There was no way Mark Antony would go along with Cicero's plans to return the Republic to the past and so he set his sights on winning over Octavian. Cicero was actively warned against this by his co-conspirators – Octavian might be inexperienced but he was known to be whip-smart and ruthless, likely to turn from a friend to an enemy if that would serve him best. However, Cicero shrugged off their remonstrations; after all, Octavian was a boy, and Cicero should be able to easily outsmart him and turn him into just the malleable makeshift monarch he needed. His puppet lined up, all Cicero needed to do was take out Mark Antony.

Cicero began a series of speeches and pamphlets, dubbed *Philippics*. The plan was to use *Philippics* to assassinate Mark Antony's character, taking a page out of Julius Caesar's book and spinning the truth to frame Antony as a tyrant in waiting and pushing forward Cicero's own agenda. On 2 September 44 BC, Cicero delivered his *First Philippic* to the Senate; he began by lovingly calling Antony his dear friend, before launching into a passive-aggressive but stealthy takedown of his character. Mark Antony was not fit to rule; he would remove any of Caesar's 'good' laws and destroy the Republic. To really emphasize his supposed terror at what damage Antony would do as a ruler, Cicero recited from a poem by Accius *'Let them hate, so long as they fear'* – this, he promised, would be the mandate Antony would rule from. Unsurprisingly, Mark Antony did not react to this well and on 19 September he gathered the Senate together again and angrily responded to Cicero, falsely accusing him of being the mastermind behind Caesar's murder. Cicero was furious and unable to contain his rage. He threw out his original plan of using *Philippics* for under-the-radar spin and instead embarked on an all-out slanderous campaign.

Second Philippic is by far the longest and most explosive of Cicero's fourteen *Philippic* instalments, an unrivalled rant: '*oh how intolerable is his impudence, his debauchery, and his lust!*' Cicero's vitriolic claims run from Antony reeking of vomit from three-day revelries to thievery, violence, and claims he was a former sex worker. Cicero does not substantiate these stories and they mostly contained little to no fact, yet they proved incendiary to Antony's character and 2,000 years later he is still thought of as a reckless philanderer.

Cicero's firebrand takedown in his *Philippics* continued into the spring of 43 BC. In April the Senate aligned with him and his false claims, announcing Antony an enemy of the state. Octavian led the Senate's forces into battle against Antony and deftly defeated Caesar's would-be successor. Victorious, Cicero delivered a jubilant speech to the people of Rome – his plan had won out and the Republic would be restored. However, he had forgotten one thing – the warnings that Octavian could not be trusted. While Cicero celebrated, Octavian and Antony had formed an alliance.

Together with Marcus Aemilius Lepidus, a long-time ally of Caesar, Octavian and Antony formed the Second Triumvirate, a military dictatorship divided between the three. As they seized power, the trio began compiling a Proscription, a list

---

SMARTED SMEARS

The *Philippics* changed the way history has viewed
Mark Antony, but it wasn't the only contemporary
assassination of his character. Octavian and Antony's
alliance was not to last, and once it crumbled,
Octavian set out on a propaganda spree against his
former ally. It's from this that we get the tales of Mark
Antony abandoning his Roman ways and falling under
the spell of the Egyptian Queen Cleopatra.

---

of those immediately condemned to death. Of course, Mark
Antony ensured that Cicero's name was on it. In December 43
BC, Cicero was beheaded, and in a further act of grisly revenge,
Antony ordered that not only would Cicero's head be displayed
at the Roman Forum, but so too would be his writing hand –
the pen no match for his sword.

ARMINIUS AND THE BATTLE OF
THE TEUTOBURG FOREST

Following the fall of Cicero came the demise of the Roman
Republic. The Second Triumvirate held on to power for just
over a decade, but by 30 BC, Octavian was the last of the
trio standing, having exiled Marcus Aemilius Lepidus and

defeated Mark Antony in a civil war. Now sole ruler, he began to strip away the Republic's democratic roots and lay down the groundwork for an imperial centralized authority that he planned to be at the centre of. In 27 BC, Octavian changed his name to Augustus and became to all intents and purposes the first Roman Emperor. The Republic was dead, long live the Roman Empire.

The first thing on Augustus's imperial agenda was to expand his new empire. This should have been an easy task; after all, he had inherited a great amount. Following the Gallic Wars, much of Gaul had remained under Roman submission; however, just as it had been for his great-uncle Caesar, Germania remained a thorn in Augustus's side. Occupying parts of modern-day Germany, Poland, the Czech Republic, Slovakia, Hungary and Austria, the Germanic tribes were seemingly invincible, continuing to fight back no matter what. The Tencteri and Usipetes tribes that had suffered such catastrophic losses in 55 BC at the hands of Caesar were back to fighting form by 17–16 BC and defeated Rome's fifth legion in battle. This loss was so brutal and embarrassing to the empire that it became known as the Lollian disaster. Augustus refused to let this stand. He wanted the Germanic tribes' land for his empire and he would get it through brute strength, so he launched a lengthy series of campaigns against Germania in 12 BC.

Born around 16 BC, Arminius was an early victim of Augustus's machinations. The son of the chief of north-western Germany's Cherusci tribe, as a child he was used as a pawn in peace negotiations with Rome and taken as their hostage. Although he grew up as a prisoner of the empire, he was afforded an education, learned to speak Latin, joined the Roman army and was even awarded the title of Knight. Meanwhile, back in Arminius's homeland, Augustus's campaigns had proved a rousing success. The Germanic tribes had been unable to hold against the might of the Roman army and by AD 7 they were securely under Rome's thumb. To make sure things stayed that way, Augustus brought in one of the empire's most ruthless leaders to take charge of Rome's new lands. General and politician Publius Quinctilius Varus was known for his cruelty and brutality. During his tenure as Governor of Syria, he'd quashed multiple crises through a mixture of deadly force and fear, a tactic he now planned to use on the Germanic people. Still, this was not a task he could undertake without local help, and who was better placed to do that than Arminius? Sure, Arminius was born into the tribes Varus was now trying to suppress, but he was seen by the Romans as 'one of us'; therefore, his insider knowledge and loyalty to Rome would be key to Varus's success.

This trust in Arminius was catastrophically misplaced. Arminius had never been on the Romans' side; he'd just been biding his time. When Varus believed that Arminius was travelling to local tribes and rallying support for Rome, he'd actually been winning their favour and planning an insurrection. It took Arminius almost two years of double-crossing, but by September AD 9 he had united multiple tribes, including his own people, the Cherusci, and was ready to fight. However,

Varus's forces were well trained, well equipped and strong. If Arminius stood any chance of winning, he'd need to plan his attack carefully.

It was Varus's belief that he and the Roman army were invincible that Arminius chose to play on. Varus had believed that Arminius would never go back to what he saw as a bunch of inferior barbarians, and it was this blind faith in his force and his man on the ground that would be his downfall. Arminius knew that the Roman army were due to be marching through an area near the narrow marshes of the Teutoburg Forest. He would lay a trap, luring Varus and his men off the beaten track with the promise of a detour. Once they were in the dense forest, they could be ambushed by the Germanic tribes – the Romans didn't know the area and wouldn't be able to use their usual fighting formations. It was the best chance of bringing them down. But, just as the plan was ready to swing into action, disaster almost struck. Arminius was betrayed by a lone Cheruscan nobleman, Segestes, who warned Varus that Arminius was plotting against him. Still, so great was Varus's trust in Arminius, he shrugged it off and when Arminius presented him with the short cut through the Teutoburg Forest, he readily agreed to it, sending himself and his men to their deaths.

The battle was bloody: the tribes encircled the Romans and trapped them within the dense forest. They had no room to move into formations and were unused to the thick mud dragging them to the ground. Realizing that defeat was imminent, Varus killed himself and was soon followed in this by most of his commanders, leaving the troops leaderless and panicked. Only a handful of survivors managed to escape, and when word reached Rome of the massacre that had just unfolded, they were shocked – surely such a defeat was impossible. The Romans had drastically overestimated themselves and underestimated those they saw as backward barbarians.

UNIFYING FORCE

Arminius became Germany's first national hero. His story was mostly lost to history until it was rediscovered in archives in the 1400s, quickly gaining traction as a symbol of a united Germany and becoming something of a national emblem during the Napoleonic Wars.

If Augustus had thought the Lollian disaster was bad, it was nothing compared to what Arminius had just pulled off. The Battle of the Teutoburg Forest was one of Rome's most devastating losses to date, wiping out an estimated 10 per cent of its Imperial Army and pushing the empire out of the land. Classical Roman historians such as Suetonius claimed that the loss almost totally destroyed belief in the burgeoning empire and emotionally crippled Augustus, who on hearing the news allegedly began hitting his head against his palace walls, desperately calling out for his lost legions.

THE SECRET HISTORY

In the third century AD, the Roman Empire began to fall into serious trouble. Built around military might and expansion, much of the empire's economic system was tied to this continual success: wealth plundered from conquered lands and free labour courtesy of prisoners of war and enforced slavery. So, once the empire halted expansion and began to suffer a series of major military losses, it wasn't just its position as a global superpower that suffered, but its bottom line too. Coupled with government corruption and the rise of Christianity eroding the influence of Rome's emperors over their people, the Roman Empire was set to fall. At least it was in the west. In 330, Emperor Constantine the Great had moved the seat of the empire to Byzantium, making a new 'Rome' of his self-titled capital city, Constantinople. When the Western Roman Empire fell in 476, its counterpart in the east – commonly known as the Byzantine Empire – was flourishing.

In the thick of this emerging power was Procopius of Caesarea, an ancient scholar and historian born in 500. It was Procopius's job to write down an ongoing account of the reign of Byzantium's first 'great' ruler, the handily titled Justinian the Great. Coming to power in 527, Justinian's reign was at times rocky, perhaps best encapsulated by the 532 Nika Riots, an uprising against Justinian that, although ultimately quashed, resulted in half of Constantinople lying in ruins and the massacre of tens of thousands of rioters. Oppressive and ambitious, much of Justinian's rule was marked by his expansion of empire and reconquest of lands that had fallen out of imperial control; Persia, North Africa and Italy were among the areas targeted. At Justinian's right hand was his wife and Empress, Theodora, at first noted for her lowly birth but later for her active role as one of Justinian's key advisers. Watching on the sidelines through all of this was Procopius – a constant presence in Justinian's court, an eyewitness to the Nika Riots and companion to Justinian's favourite general, Belisarius, on his numerous military campaigns.

Everything Procopius had seen was encapsulated in two of his three books: *History of the Wars* and *The Buildings*. These would become the most known accounts of the reign of Justinian the Great, and as they were written under his watchful eye, it's unsurprising that they offer a mostly flattering rendition. Justinian and Theodora are pious and righteous rulers, and following the example of Caesar's *Commentaries*, Justinian's actions are almost always justified – even when they result in tragic bloodshed. Procopius had set in stone the history of Justinian, and his writings remained undisputed fact until the early 1600s, when a mysterious manuscript was found deep within the annals of the Vatican library. On translating the document from its original Greek into Latin, antiquarian Niccolò Alamanni discovered that this wasn't your run-of-the-mill accidentally mislaid archival object; it was a hitherto unknown third book of Procopius titled *Anecdota* or *Secret History*.

To say that nobody anticipated how explosive the book's contents would be is a vast understatement. *Secret History* upended what historians thought they knew about Justinian's reign, with Procopius starting the book by explaining that much of what he'd written up to that point had been a lie: '*I have been forced to conceal the real causes of many of the events recounted in my former books. It will now be my duty, in this part of my history, to tell what has hitherto remained untold, and to state the real motives and origin of the actions which I have already recounted.*' Adultery, abortions, secret children, murder, corruption and deceit all played major roles in Procopius's retelling.

Particular aim is taken at Theodora, who Procopius claims was a former sex worker. Indeed, he goes into such lurid details of her rumoured sex life that the 1623 publication of *Secret History* actually edited those portions out. As a couple, Justinian and Theodora are likened to demons: '... *scourges of mankind, who laid their heads together to see how they could fastest and most easily destroy the race and the works of man*'. Procopius even suggests that the couple may in fact have been literal demons, with deities fighting back against their ungodly reign by unleashing plagues and natural disasters on the empire. Of Justinian's campaigns of reconquest Procopius is predictably unrestrained in his critique, claiming that from what he witnessed the emperor was responsible for the deaths of millions of people, with 5 million in Mauretania alone '*exterminated*'.

Investigations into the book have found that it is almost certain Procopius was the author; however, how much of what he wrote is true is still up for debate. Of course, Justinian and

Theodora were not demons undercover as humans plotting to destroy the world; however, beyond those kinds of nonsensical claims, a lot of truth can be found – but only once we strip back Procopius's own biases. For example, was Theodora a former sex worker? The evidence would suggest so. From her childhood, Theodora worked in theatre, where many actresses also engaged in sex work and forcible trafficking of young girls like Theodora was prevalent. Procopius uses this as the key reason for his claims of Theodora's evil nature and her spread of sexual debauchery. However, we can see from his contemporaries that Procopius is deliberately leaving out key details that would somewhat undermine his portrayal of Theodora – primarily that once in power Theodora took up the mantle of bettering women's rights, including working to help prevent the forcible trafficking of girls into sexual slavery. As for the claims that Justinian's campaigns were far bloodier than first described – this is almost certainly true. However, the huge number of fatalities that Procopius cites is likely nothing more than conjecture.

The *Secret History* is Procopius's own version of the truth and as when any of us recall our own history, it is to an extent fictionalized, mixing rumour with what we've witnessed, personal bias with fact. Perhaps the best thing to do is view *History of the Wars*, *The Buildings* and *Secret History* as a trilogy – the first two instalments a commissioned tribute to Procopius's boss and the third a rampant release of his real feelings towards that boss. Each volume is biased in its own way, offering only one version of events and at points mixing fact with fiction to get the desired outcome. Allowing us perhaps not a reliable glimpse into history, but one of how history is told – the official versus the personal.

Part II

THE MIDDLE AGES

THE CRIMES OF EMPRESS WU

China's Tang dynasty is often called the Golden Age of Ancient China, and at the helm of one of its most illustrious turning points was Wu Zetian, the only woman in Chinese dynastic history to rule not as a dowager or consort, but as empress in her own right. During her 690–705 reign, Wu expanded the empire, reopened the Silk Road and funnelled government funding into endeavours to care for the poor and sick. Prior to her death in 705, Empress Wu chose to leave her grave's epitaph blank, wanting her reign to be judged only by history. This *may* not have been such a good idea. History has not remembered Wu as a strong and effective ruler, but as a callous murderer, who would later be described in this way: '*She killed her sister, slaughtered her brothers, murdered her emperor, and poisoned her mother. Both gods and humans hate her.*'

The crimes laid at the feet of Empress Wu are some of the most heinous you'll find in any history book. Wu began her career as a concubine, first for Emperor Taizong and then for Emperor Gaozong. In 654, she gave birth to Gaozong's child and allegedly killed the baby so she could frame the emperor's wife, Empress Wang, and former favourite consort, Xiao, for murder and sorcery, resulting in their grisly deaths and her rise to Empress Consort. Then in 675, another of Wu's children suddenly died, this time her eldest son, Li Hong, whose demise happened *just* after an argument with his mother. When Emperor Gaozong died in 683, Wu was again linked to his death, alongside a now considerable bloody trail of her own family members – cousins, nieces and nephews who'd posed a threat and mysteriously died or been accused of treason. The familial murder spree petered out once Wu became Dowager Empress; however, she still wasn't winning any mother of the year awards. Wu used her remaining sons as puppet rulers; when one got out of hand, she'd simply depose and exile him, replacing him with a more docile sibling, until finally in 690 her youngest son, Emperor Ruizong, abdicated to make way for the sole rule of Empress Wu.

But how much of this is true? There is a saying that history is written by the victors; however, history is also written by those that would like to be seen as the victors and that's almost certainly the case here. Following the end of the Tang dynasty, China entered a fifty-year period of turmoil known as the Five Dynasties and Ten Kingdoms period. Without a central authority, this was a chaotic time, to say the least, and when the Song dynasty began in 960, it was an uphill battle to return China to the state it had been in during the Tang and Han dynasties. This resulted in an effort to promote Chinese identity and revive Confucianism, not only in day-to-day life but in the telling of China's history. The problem was that the reign of Empress Wu did not fit into this narrative, as explained by contemporary Song scholar Zhu Xi: '*The Tang dynasty originated from the Barbarians. It is for this reason that violations of the Confucian standard of governing a woman's proper behaviour were not regarded as anything unusual.*'

THE MISTRESS

Wu Zetian entered the Imperial Harem for Emperor Taizong at the age of fourteen. Although a concubine, she was not favoured by him; however, she formed a relationship with the soon-to-be Emperor Gaozong during Taizong's fatal illness. It appears this coupling was encouraged by Gaozong's wife, Empress Wang, in a bid to pull him away from his favourite concubine, Consort Xiao.

Empress Wu's achievements and length of reign meant that she could not be relegated to the corners of history, but she was not the kind of woman that Song historians wanted to be celebrated. It was much simpler to cherry-pick what parts of Wu's history to include and to focus on accounts from those that opposed her reign. The earlier quote of *'Both gods and humans hate her'* is to this day one of the most used quotes about Empress Wu, yet it was one of the most biased contemporary accounts of her, that of poet Luo Binwang, and was written to gain support for a rebellion against Wu. As with Cicero's *Philippics*, these kinds of vitriolic takedowns aren't always the most credible historical sources. Yet in the histories of Empress Wu written during the Song period, these were frequently the only kinds of accounts used – meaning that much of what is framed as fact was often just rumour and speculation.

Did Empress Wu kill her baby, son and husband? It's unlikely. There are multiple accounts from Wu's lifetime that state that Li Hong had a long-term illness from childhood (likely tuberculosis) and it was this that caused his death. Similarly, Emperor Gaozong had a debilitating stroke in 660, which led to ill health for the rest of his life. As for Wu's baby, there is little concrete evidence from her life to suggest that Wu killed her child, and accounts of the killing from Song historians ratchet up the level of brutality in the alleged murder throughout each retelling.

That's not to say Wu was a wholly innocent party who has been completely demonized by history. Even if she didn't kill her baby, she did use her own child's death to frame two innocent women and then oversaw their executions. Likewise, she almost certainly had a hand in the deaths and accusations made towards those members of her extended family that posed a potential threat. To put it bluntly, Empress Wu was as ruthless in gaining power as she was effective in her reign. Yet, despite in the latter being arguably one of the Tang dynasty's greatest emperors, Wu's achievements remain relatively unremembered. Perhaps this is an example of history taking the easy route. It's simpler to go by the histories of the Song Dynasties and see Wu as the bloodthirsty villain rather than digging deeper into the profoundly complex ruler she truly was.

MAGIC AND MONMOUTH

Around 1135, cleric and writer Geoffrey of Monmouth published a book that flipped every conceived notion of British history on its head. *Historia Regum Brittaniae / De gestis Britonum* (simply known today as *The History of the Kings of Britain*) would become a medieval bestseller. It was read across Europe and the Byzantine Empire and used by English scholars through to the sixteenth century. What made the book so important? Monmouth had uncovered a chapter of history that had never been seen in any other major historical work – the history of King Arthur and Merlin. Alongside this lost Arthurian history were accounts of ancient giants who once roamed British shores and the lives of King Lear and Cymbeline. Of course, almost nothing about Monmouth's amazing discovery was true – but few apart from Monmouth knew that.

It's easy to see why people believed Monmouth as he came up with an incredibly compelling story behind his find. According to Monmouth, during his scholarly pursuits, he began to realize that there was a huge gap in recorded British history both before and after '*the incarnation of Christ*'. While hunting down these forgotten chapters in time, his friend the Archdeacon of Oxford told him of an '*ancient book*' that handily contained all those missing pieces he was looking for – '*from Brutus the first king of Britons down to Cadwallader son of Cadwallo*', as well as a series of prophecies by Merlin which foretold Britain's future. *The History* was Monmouth's direct translation of this book into Latin (then the learned language of the day), and his introduction to the manuscript is littered with mentions of England's great and good who he counts as patrons of his work. All of this combined gave Monmouth's work the illusion of truth. It didn't appear to be an out-of-the-blue fake; it was written by a scholar, in Latin, with numerous individuals' backing – of course it was believed.

Academics quickly began incorporating *The History* into their own works, but there were a few naysayers – after all, nobody but Monmouth had seen the mythical tome his work was based on, which alone is fairly suspicious. One of these doubters was historian William of Newburgh, whose own work *Historia rerum Anglicarum (History of English Affairs)* was something of a contemporary rival to *The History*. In the preface to his book, Newburgh tears into Monmouth: '*impudently he falsifies in every respect*', outlining how few of the sources Monmouth cites actually exist. This is certainly true and Newburgh's works contain a lot more factually accurate information; however, he too indulges in the fanciful, including stories of ghosts and the undead, which make his arguments against Monmouth's fantastical Arthurian world a little harder to swallow. The other prominent critic of *The History* at the time was Gerald of Wales, a secular clerk and historian. In perhaps the most medieval of put-downs, Gerald wrote a story in which tiny devils would appear all over a man when he was confronted with lies, his condition at its worst when Monmouth's book was placed on his lap.

As time went on, more focus was put on *The History*'s inclusion of Merlin's prophecies. Monmouth wrote hundreds of these prophecies, which he attributed to Merlin, running from the pretty clear to the vague, verging on nonsensical, for example: '*The Hedgehog will hide its apples inside Winchester and will construct hidden passages under the earth.*' In the Middle Ages and early modern period, great stock was placed in these prophecies, and their often hazy language meant that they could easily be attributed to anything; for example, two English kings, Henry II (1154–89) and Edward III (1327–77), claimed to be embodiments of boars that Merlin foretold would save the English people. Similar use of such tenuous links can even be found as late as 1603, when James I succeeded Elizabeth I and stated that this too had been prophesied by Merlin.

That's not to say that every single aspect of *The History* is a total lie. Historian and archaeologist Miles Russell argues in his revaluation of the work he found that beyond the tales of wizards and giants, Monmouth utilized a whole host of credible sources from the south-east of England, which dated back as far as the first century BC. These, according to Russell, provide a new way of understanding how ancient Britons lived and thought. Helping provide new takes on historic events, such as British tribes helping the Romans quell Boudica's uprising in AD 60 or the Romans tampering with Stonehenge and potentially making their own additions.

THE MAGIC OF MERLIN

The History of the Kings of Britain laid the groundwork that future Arthurian writers, such as Marie de France and Sir Thomas Malory, would build upon, with Monmouth defining King Arthur's personality and family history, as well as his strong ties to Merlin.

Still, eventually, *The History* began to fall out of favour, as scholars started to realize how much of a massive jump in logic needed to be taken to read the whole book at face value – William of Newburgh and Gerald of Wales were now being taken seriously, albeit centuries too late. In 1718, one Aaron Thompson published the first English translation of *The History* and was so worried that by reprinting Monmouth's writing he'd be opening a Pandora's box of misinformation that he included a hefty tome of an introduction, going to great pains to remind the reader that *The History* is: '*barbarous and in many places obscure*'.

We'll likely never know why Geoffrey of Monmouth included so much fabrication in his history of Britain. Still, it's perhaps one of history's most impressive lies and still impacts our lives today. The debate on whether King Arthur was real rages on, though with little concrete evidence that he was. Interestingly though, there are accounts of a ninth-century warlord and tenth-century Welsh leader with that name, which is possibly where Monmouth got the inspiration for his fictional version. Slightly redundant historic arguments aside, the cultural legacy of *The History* is almost as unbelievable as its source material, spanning two Shakespeare plays, as well as countless books, films and TV shows that have built on the Arthurian legend. Geoffrey of Monmouth may still be seen by many to be a pseudo-historian, but his lies make him perhaps one of the greatest fiction writers of all time.

THE FALL OF THE KOMNENOI

When the Byzantine Emperor Alexios I Komnenos died in 1118, he was heralded as having achieved the impossible, saving the empire from collapsing into oblivion. Just a century earlier under the reign of Basil II, Byzantium was a force to be reckoned with, the dominant power in the Baltics and Middle East, but Basil's death in 1025 had triggered a battle for succession. No ruler would last for more than a few years before infighting, coups and revolts caused another shift in power. By the time Alexios I came to the throne in 1081, many of the empire's borders had been breached. Turkish nomads were settling in Anatolia and Normans were merrily plundering their Italian lands. Miraculously, in the decades that followed, Alexios would turn this around, raising Byzantium from its knees. When he died, the empire may have been territorially smaller but its economic health and military might were vastly improved. He'd also cemented in place his hereditary dynasty of the Komnenoi. No more would wars of succession derail the empire – now back to being a great power, it would only grow under a steady Komnenoi hand. At least that was the plan.

To begin with, things went extremely well for the new-found dynasty, and the growth that had begun under Alexios continued through the reigns of John II Komnenos and then Manuel I Komnenos. However, Manuel's reign was somewhat marked by his overambitious nature. When he came to the throne, the empire was the biggest power in the Mediterranean, but only by a hair. If Manuel wanted to cement the Komnenoi hold, he needed allies. For this, he looked to powerhouses under the umbrella of the Holy Roman Emperor, enjoying alliances with Conrad III of Germany and Béla III of Hungary. Yet allegiances would shift when Conrad died in 1152. Manuel had been planning a campaign with Conrad that would carve up Italy between Byzantium and Germany and return Sicily to the empire's rule. However, Germany's new king, Frederick Barbarossa, was quick to withdraw his support, a situation only made worse when in 1155 Frederick was crowned Holy Roman Emperor. Frederick wanted Italy, Manuel wanted Italy and Sicily, while the Sicilian king, William II of Sicily, just wanted everyone to back off from his land.

At the same time as that disaster was unravelling, Manuel was grappling with a family crisis in the form of his cousin, Andronikos Komnenos. The pair had grown up together, but in 1153 Manuel learned that Andronikos had become involved in a plot to overthrow him. Andronikos was imprisoned but escaped in 1165, later fleeing to the Crusader state of Antioch. After years of fighting, Byzantium and Antioch had just brokered an alliance thanks to Manuel's marriage to Maria of Antioch. However, when Andronikos slept with the Prince of Antioch's youngest daughter, Philippa, and took her as his mistress, the tenuous peace was shaken. Fearing the wrath of his cousin, Andronikos fled to Jerusalem, where in 1167 he embarked on yet another affair, this time with the recently widowed former Queen of Jerusalem, Theodora Komnene, who also happened to be Manuel's niece. The lovers made a break for it, eventually settling on the Byzantine border where they formed their own thief kingdom and pushed for Andronikos to take the crown. In response, Manuel seized Theodora and the couple's children and, in 1180, forced Andronikos to swear his loyalty in return for their release. Andronikos was then exiled into retirement – a threat that would surely never appear again.

The dynastic line was safe, but the empire was not. In addition to the tensions between Byzantium, the Holy Roman Emperor and William II of Sicily, in 1175 Manuel had broken his alliance with the Seljuk Turks, resulting in a back-and-forth war. Although it had not been an utter failure, it had shown how entrenched the Turks were within Asia Minor. When

A BLINDING NICKNAME

The twelfth-century Byzantine historian Nicetas Choniata gave Andronikos I Komnenos the nickname 'Hater of Sunlight' for how often he blinded his enemies as punishment.

Manuel died in 1180, it was clear that although Byzantium was still strong, it would need a steady leader to navigate through its current crises. Unfortunately, that leader was an eleven-year-old boy. Alexios II was the son of Manuel and Maria of Antioch. Due to his young age, he obviously couldn't lead and so whilst he spent his time playing sports and hunting, his mother and her new lover, Alexios Komnenos (known as Alexios the Protosebastos), would rule as de facto regent. Alexios was not a good man for this job, more concerned with lining his own pockets than the running of the empire. In turn, the couple began to show far more favour towards emigrated citizens from the republics of Pisa and Genoa, who became part of what was known as a Latin minority. As corruption became rooted and rumours of plots to assassinate Alexios the Protosebastos flourished, Andronikos Komnenos emerged once more. In 1182, Andronikos formed an army and marched on Constantinople. When he got there, the city quickly turned to his side; Alexios the Protosebastos was blinded and forced to enter a monastery, while Maria of Antioch was confined to a nunnery. To deepen the loyalty of the city's mob who'd come to his aid, Andronikos permitted a massacre in Constantinople's Latin quarter. Thousands were killed, and women, children and the sick were not spared, with the Orthodox clergy even delivering victims to the mob. As a result, many alliances and communications between Byzantium and Western Europe crumbled, with countries unable to fathom the bloodshed that Andronikos had overseen.

In the midst of this was Alexios II, still technically the ruler. Andronikos chose not to depose him, instead having the boy crowned anew in May 1182, where he swore his allegiance and protection of Alexios. With the young emperor under his control, Andronikos began picking off those who might threaten his new-found power. A likely falsified conspiracy was created to bring down Maria of Antioch, Andronikos forcing Alexios to sign his own mother's death warrant. Following this, Andronikos began a reign of terror against the nobility, often using trumped-up charges and framed crimes to have them blinded, exiled or killed. In September 1183, Andronikos announced yet another coronation – he would become co-emperor. After once more swearing his lifelong loyalty to Alexios II, Andronikos began plotting how to murder the boy. That same month, the new co-emperor declared himself the one true ruler, tasking his friends with the strangulation of young Alexios. The sole reign of Andronikos I had officially begun.

The rule of Andronikos would be one of an iron fist, symbolized by his legions of spies, disappearances of enemies in the night, and some of the most brutal public executions within historic record. Focused on his tyrannical reign at home, Andronikos failed to prevent the rising threats approaching his borders. In 1185, William II of Sicily embarked on an invasion of Byzantium. Meanwhile, Andronikos was busy plotting the extermination of his nobility. In August, when William's forces sacked the city of Thessalonica, resulting in the massacre of thousands, Andronikos tried to make light of the situation – it was fine, cities had fallen before, it was no big deal. Unsurprisingly, this flippant take didn't go down well and as his people turned against him, Andronikos ordered the executions of anyone who he saw as a traitor. Among this number was Isaac Angelus, a nobleman who'd previously been involved in uprisings against the Crown and was known for his inability to lead. In early September 1185, officials were sent to Isaac's home in Constantinople to arrest him; however, after a fight, Isaac escaped and took refuge at a nearby shrine. By the next morning, word had begun spreading through the city of Andronikos's latest planned arrests, and now thoroughly fed up with his rule, a mob quickly formed, calling for Isaac to take the throne. Isaac baulked at the idea – he didn't want to be emperor, but the mob demanded it and a kind of semi-forced coronation took place.

As Isaac was crowned, Isaac II Angelus, the last of the Komnenoi fled, hoping to seek a safe harbour in Russia. However, Andronikos was quickly captured and sentenced to a barbaric execution, first beaten by surviving nobility, before being paraded through Constantinople and hung by his feet at the Hippodrome, where a baying mob was set loose on him. The Komnenoi dynasty once heralded as saviours of the empire was dead. In many ways, Andronikos himself had destroyed both it and any chance of a steady dynasty curtailing the demise of the Byzantine Empire. Under Isaac's short-lived lineage – the Angelus dynasty – Byzantium would endure some of its mightiest blows, including the partitioning of the empire in 1204. That same year, the Komnenoi would technically rule once more, with Andronikos's grandsons Alexios and David founding the successor state, the Empire of Trebizond. Yet, the glory days would never be recaptured and neither they, nor any Komnenoi, would rule over Constantinople again. As for the empire itself, it would never fully recover, thanks in no small part to the lies and the corruption that seeded the reign of Andronikos.

The Betrayal of the Knights Templar

Known today as a crack Catholic military order, the Knights Templar actually began life as a kind of roadside assistance for pilgrims. Between 1096 and 1099, the First Crusade had seen Christian forces from Western Europe wage war on Jerusalem and the 'Holy Land' in a bid to claim it back from Islamic rule. Now under Christian occupation, pilgrims flocked to Jerusalem and the holy sites around it. However, the area was highly dangerous; the First Crusade had been incredibly bloody and the tactics used by crusaders were often beyond brutal, leading Christian pilgrims to become a target – soon their bodies were piling up on the roads to Jerusalem.

Around 1118, French knight Hugues de Payens came up with a solution, rallying together friends and family to create a small order that would protect pilgrims on their journeys. This order relied almost entirely on donations to operate, but luckily, their aims quickly made them a favourite religious charitable pursuit and within just a few years the once minor band of knights weren't only being showered with cash, but with a flood of eager new recruits. In 1139, the Knights Templar became somewhat of an unstoppable force after they were given papal backing – allowing them tax exemption, free travel between borders, and the declaration that nobody had governance over them, other than the pope.

Throughout the 1200s, the Templars were a vivid emblem

of the Christian crusades – an army with God on their side who could never be defeated. It wasn't just their reputation that was on the rise though. War proved very good business for the Templars. Although technically its members lived monastic lives of poverty, the order itself grew staggeringly wealthy. Those early donations had snowballed and the Knights Templar now had their own empire of land, estates and wealth, even organizing an economic system to allow vast movements of cash between territories. In many ways, they'd become a kind of medieval bank, with countries like France borrowing money to beef up their own forces during crusades. Now one of the financial powerhouses of Europe, the Knights Templar had significantly strayed from their original purpose, but none of that necessarily mattered as long as they were successful in crusades and keeping both donors and debtors happy – but of course, that winning streak ended.

Perhaps the biggest blow was the Fall of Acre in 1291, when the Mamluk Sultanate successfully laid siege to the last great crusader stronghold in the Kingdom of Jerusalem. The Templars had been unable to hold back the vast invading force and included in the many fatalities was Knights Templar Grand Master, William of Beaujeu. The Fall of Acre effectively spelled the end of the Templars' heyday and amidst a series of subsequent defeats they were thrown out of the Holy Land. The superstitious mystique that once surrounded 'God's army' was broken – they were not invincible and, perhaps worse still, they were wholly susceptible to human foibles. Rumours of Templar misdeeds had been swirling for a few decades already, with chroniclers William of Tyre and Matthew Paris accusing the order of corruption and greed, Paris even going so far as suggesting that Templars had at times sabotaged their own missions to eke out the length of crusades and earn more money.

On seriously shaky ground, the Templars began to plan how to launch yet another crusade and win back favour. In 1306, Templar Grand Master Jacques de Molay was called to France to meet with Pope Clement V to discuss the proposed crusade. However, the timing for this meeting was not great. The King of France, Philip IV, had begun to get increasingly frustrated with the Knights Templar. For one thing, he was heavily in debt to them, and for another, Molay was pushing back against Philip's hopes to merge the Templars with other orders, creating a kind of super crusading machine that would operate under the French king's control. Adding even more fuel to this fire, after Molay arrived in France around late 1306, an ousted Templar accused the order of heresy. This was a serious allegation and to make matters worse, the planned crusade talks were put on hold after Clement V became ill. By late June 1307, the heresy claims had gained so much traction that Molay met with Philip IV to plead the innocence of the order. Yet Philip wasn't having it. Whether or not he believed the accusations, it was the straw that broke the camel's back. The Templars had been a thorn in his side for too long; they weren't serving their original purpose, they wouldn't play ball and he was much in debt – they had to go.

On 13 October 1307, Philip IV ordered the arrest of every Knights Templar member in France. The heresy accusations were at the heart of this, but to bring down the whole order Philip would need more, so allegations were built upon and hastily invented. For example, it was known that order members would exchange a 'kiss of peace' on the lips. This singular piece of evidence was mutated to accuse the order of ritualistic sodomy. To gain the confessions Philip wanted, order members weren't just interrogated but tortured, leading to a slew of false confessions – even Molay confessed to defacing a crucifix and denying Christ. In all, an estimated thirty-six Templars died under torture, refusing to admit to the charges. Of the other 138 Templar testimonies, all but four were confessions.

Despite the pope officially being the only authority above the Templars, Clement V didn't seem able to stop Philip IV, and at times played into his hands. In November 1307, Clement released a papal bull, *Pastoralis praeeminentiae*, ordering all Christian kingdoms to arrest Templars and conduct their own investigations. Interestingly, in the countries that didn't use torture in their interrogations, such as Cyprus and England, confessions were incredibly rare. Still, Philip continued his campaign and in 1308 published *Articles of Accusation*, a list not only of the charges confessed to by the Templars but of accusations that ranged from invading the religious rights of churches and bishops to hiding their actions from the papal authority. Seemingly two steps behind, Clement wrote to Philip and accused him of destroying the Templars' reputation – of course he was! That was exactly what Philip wanted, having *Articles of Accusation* read in town and village squares in a bid to further turn people against the Templars.

By now many of the Knights Templar arrested in France had recanted their confessions and Clement V was pushing for trials for them. In response in May 1310, Philip ordered the executions of fifty-four Templars, burning the men at the stake. For the remaining Knights, they would be allowed to live *if* they stood by their original confessions – a route many took. The Knights Templar were now beyond saving. Their reputation was in ruins, and keeping them around as an extension of the Catholic Church was no longer tenable. In 1312, Clement V officially dissolved the order. Two years later, in March 1314, Jacques de Molay was burned at the stake after he recanted his confession. This led to a long-lasting legend that in his dying breaths Molay cursed those that had bought down his order – within a year both Clement V and Philip IV were dead.

UNLUCKY FOR SOME

The Knights Templar are entrenched in multiple historic myths including that the superstition of Friday the 13th being unlucky came from their arrest in 1307. This is not true, as the origins of the belief reach far further back, including biblical references to the Last Supper, where Judas was the thirteenth guest, and Norse mythology, which had another thirteenth guest, Loki, ruin a party by plunging the world into darkness.

But this wouldn't be the end of the story. Almost 700 years later, in 2001, a lost document was uncovered in the Vatican Archives, and much like the discovery of Procopius's *Secret History*, this would be a game-changer. Palaeographer Barbara Frale found the Chinon Parchment, a document long assumed to exist but until that point lost to history, thanks to a long-forgotten archiver accidentally cataloguing it incorrectly. The parchment shows that in 1308, following a papal investigation, Clement had actually absolved the Knights Templar of any charges of heresy, finding them innocent but in need of reform. Philip IV had ignored this and marched on regardless, spinning a web of lies and knowingly killing innocent men for his own gain.

JEANNE AND THE BLACK FLEET

In the years immediately following the death of Philip IV, France had hit a rocky patch. Philip's son, Charles IV of France, had taken over the throne; however, when he died in 1328, he left no male heirs, leaving the crown somewhat up for grabs. The two frontrunners for the position of king were Charles's cousin Philip, and Charles's nephew Edward – who just so happened to be King Edward III of England. As a more direct blood relation, Edward arguably had the stronger claim, but fortunately for Philip at the time of Charles IV's death, Edward wasn't really in a position to skirmish for succession.

Just one year into his reign, the sixteen-year-old king was at loggerheads with his mother's lover, Roger Mortimer, who was using Edward's age as an excuse to seize power for himself. With Edward essentially out of the picture, Philip was crowned King of France.

But the battle for the crown was far from over; for centuries England and France had been fighting over who owned what chunks of land. This began in 1066 when the Dukes of Normandy, led by William the Conqueror, seized England, and as this new Anglo-French dynasty progressed it consumed more of France. By the reign of Henry II (1154–89), England had a claim to almost half of France's land. Unfortunately for Edward, by the time he came to the throne, France had taken back all of it, bar Gascony in the south-west. Fast forward to 1337 and Philip decided he wanted Gascony too. But Edward was no longer the under-the-thumb boy-king he had once been – in 1330 he had ambushed and executed Mortimer and was now making a name for himself as a fierce military ruler. So, when Philip made his bid for Gascony, Edward wasn't having it – enough was enough, he wouldn't be pushed around any longer. He might have missed out on the French throne a decade earlier, but technically his claim was still valid and so Edward didn't just want to keep Gascony, he wanted to take France. This began what is known today as the Hundred Years' War.

An early battleground was the fight to take control of France's Duchy of Brittany. The French backed Charles of Blois, while England's man was John of Montfort. Fighting for

Blois was French nobleman Olivier de Clisson, who owned a swathe of lands in Brittany. In 1342, Clisson was captured by the English and held for ransom. Likely wanting Clisson's land for himself, Charles of Blois made a play – he paid off Clisson's ransom, but then accused Clisson of being a traitor, citing that the English had made the ransom suspiciously low. The French nobility were shocked at the claims laid before Clisson – he was, after all, one of Charles's most loyal men and there was no concrete evidence against him. Nonetheless, in August 1343, Olivier de Clisson was beheaded for treason, much of his land and wealth going to Charles of Blois and Philip VI. Clisson had been framed, but trumping up charges in the name of power and wealth was nothing new, and neither Charles nor Philip expected any consequences. Sadly, they didn't count on one thing – Olivier de Clisson had left a widow – France had accidentally just created its very own supervillain.

THE LONG WAR

The Hundred Years' War lasted from 1337 to 1453, meaning that despite the name, the longest war in European history actually lasted 112 years. Alongside Jeanne, the war would include many famous faces and events, including the Battle of Agincourt and the rise and demise of Joan of Arc.

Prior to her husband's death, Jeanne de Clisson had lived a life fairly typical of a French noblewoman. Born in 1300, she had first been married off at twelve and endured two loveless marriages, before marrying Olivier in 1330. Their marriage had been a rarity for the time, in that the pair were actually in love, living happily together with their children on Brittany's border. However, when Olivier was executed, Jeanne didn't do what was expected – instead of using what little money was left to move away and live quietly, she vowed revenge on Charles of Blois and Philip VI. Jeanne sold everything that wasn't nailed down and used the money to raise a small army. Her first target was a castle being managed by Galois de la Heuse, a friend of Charles of Blois. Allegedly, in the middle of the night, Jeanne appeared at the castle gates surrounded by her children and begged to be let in. Of course, the gates were opened for this poor woman in distress, at which point Jeanne's army flooded in behind her. The castle's occupants were slaughtered, their goods stolen, and – in what would become a marker for Jeanne – one survivor left alive to tell the story.

As Jeanne continued her rampage across Brittany, she allied herself with Charles's foe, John of Montfort. With the English now backing her, Jeanne had become an even bigger threat and French forces were sent to dispatch her. With the heat too high in France, Jeanne hot-footed it across the Channel to England. Edward III was well aware of Jeanne and her bloody vengeance spree and wanted to help her however he could; after all, any enemy of Philip VI was a friend to him. Still, if Jeanne returned to France, it was highly likely that she'd meet the same fate as her husband. A plan B was hatched – Jeanne would move her revenge tour to the high seas. Three warships were purchased, painted black and their sails dyed blood red. Jeanne and her men set forth in the newly monikered Black Fleet. Jeanne's ships mostly stayed within the English Channel and there they would lie in wait for French merchant ships. Once in their sights, the ships would move in for a swift attack, butchering the crew but always sparing a few to return to France and tell their tale. By targeting merchant and supply ships, Jeanne was engaging in an early form of something called commerce raiding, a naval tactic to bring an enemy to its knees by blocking trade, logistics and aid. Jeanne and her Black Fleet did this for an estimated thirteen years.

Even when Philip VI died in 1350, Jeanne did not stop, although much as it did for the Hundred Years' War, Europe's Black Death pandemic did appear to lessen her campaign around 1348–51. Ironically, what finally seems to have ended Jeanne's reign of terror was love. In 1356, Jeanne married again, this time to an English knight, Walter Bentley. Jeanne chose to return to life as a wife, retiring her sails and in a surprising turn, moving back to Brittany. The couple settled in the coastal town of Hennebont, where in 1359 they died within weeks of each other. A quiet end for the woman once known as the Lioness of Brittany.

THE TRAVELS OF SIR JOHN MANDEVILLE

If today you were to pick up a copy of medieval travel guide *The Travels of Sir John Mandeville*, you might be understandably perplexed. Published around the mid-1300s, the purported autobiographical globetrotting guide of an English knight offered readers a glimpse of far-flung lands such as Asia and Africa, alongside accounts of parts of the world unknown – fantastical lands where griffins fly, cyclopes roam and men have hooves for feet and heads for torsos. Obviously, none of this was real. The book was essentially a hoax and even its supposed author, Sir John Mandeville, didn't actually exist. But when it was published, it was seen as fact and much like the work of Geoffrey of Monmouth, became an international bestseller. In fact, it's said that Christopher Columbus used Mandeville as a reference before sailing off to the New World. Yet it's not the idea of Columbus's confusion at not finding griffins on his travels that makes Mandeville's book so fascinating – it's how it shaped the idea of different cultures.

The *Travels of Sir John Mandeville* is in many ways a book of two halves. Much of the first half is a whistle-stop tour around Europe en route to Jerusalem and the Holy Land. Here we don't find much in the way of magical myth making, likely thanks to the fact that Mandeville lifted most of his information from other medieval pilgrim guides. So, although Mandeville may never have set foot in these countries, the authors whose work he was using did, meaning it's for the most part factual (though Mandeville being Mandeville, there are some strange inclusions, such as Noah's Ark being a kind of medieval tourist destination). Predictably, this pilgrimage section is a love letter to Western Christianity, littered with biblical references and metaphors. It's through this religious lens that Mandeville introduces the idea of 'otherness'. People that, like him, are white and Western, yet somehow incredibly different to his personal idea of what is right. This is most notable when it comes to Mandeville's 'travels' in Greece, where he meets people of the Greek Orthodox faith, noting that '*men of Greece be Christian yet they vary from our faith*'. Fascinated by this difference, Mandeville enters into a long section dissecting how their version of Christianity differs from his own – though makes it clear he believes they are wrong: '*God amend it for his mercy!*'.

These kinds of religious differences are the most prominent cultural markers in the first half of the book. Mandeville holds everyone he meets up to his own ideal of white Western Christianity. Yet, as 'strange' as he may find their lives, he saw religion as a way to bridge their cultural differences. Sadly, he did not mean this in a wholly inclusive way. Different stripes of Christianity, like Greek Orthodoxy, may be wrong in Mandeville's eyes – but their religion includes Jesus Christ. It's the same for the Muslims that he meets, as within Islam Jesus is thought of as a prophet. To Mandeville, this is a sign that they can be 'saved', converted to his version of Christianity and the '*strangeness*' of their cultures changed to that of his own Christian West. Mandeville urges his reader to tolerate their unfamiliar cultures, because one day (with the help of a little light crusading) they may change to the 'right' one.

ILLUSTRATING A LIE

Today, *The Travels of Sir John Mandeville* is mostly known for its startling woodcut illustrations of some of the more fantastical people and creatures Mandeville claimed to have met. These didn't accompany the original manuscript, but were added in the 1400s, most prominently in French and German publications, with English editions copying them.

This kind of tolerant intolerance isn't handed out to everyone though. Mandeville writes that no common ground can ever be found with those who practise Judaism. Demonization of Jewish people starts from the book's first paragraph and continues right through to the end. This kind of anti-Semitic rhetoric was nothing new – the rise of Christianity was at odds with Judaism and as one religion snowballed in popularity, the other became a target for persecution. In 1215, a papal edict demanded Jewish people must wear distinguishable badges. In 1290, Edward I ordered the expulsion of Jews from England, and during Europe's Black Death there were massacres across the continent after Jewish people were blamed for the pandemic. Mandeville was playing up to an already existing set of beliefs, but he chose to double down, claiming that during his travels he learned that Judaism was the ultimate threat: '*they shall go out in the time of anti-Christ, and that they shall make great slaughter of Christian men.*'

This final condemnation of Judaism comes in the book's second half, which focuses on the world beyond Jerusalem and pilgrims' trails. It's this section that contains the most ludicrous lies, the made-up lands of giants and men with eyes in their shoulders. Many of Mandeville's readers would never have set foot outside their own country, which is partly what made it so easy for Mandeville to lie and get away with it. He writes that in Ethiopia, many people's lower bodies are made up of one really big foot that they run around on. That the children there are born with yellow skin that turns to black as they age. It's ridiculous, but not necessarily for the average medieval reader – they had never been to Ethiopia, and they likely didn't know anybody from Ethiopia, so why couldn't this be true? Still, despite the absurdity of their depiction, Mandeville groups Ethiopians as part of those that can be 'saved', as the

Bible states that one of the Three Kings at Jesus's birth was from Ethiopia.

Yet this patronizing idea of inclusion is ditched once Mandeville leaves Ethiopia and claims to have come across a series of islands whose inhabitants, much like Jewish people, are far too different to be tolerated – this time, though, it's not religious differences, but that they are alien; '*monstrous*'. These are the lands of cyclops and hoof-footed men. All are of course made up and almost comical in their silliness, but behind that is something far more insidious. Once he has gone through these strange and often barbaric isles, Mandeville finds the safety of a kingdom where the land is rich and the people '*are white*'. From here, Mandeville returns to the theme of the book's first half – meeting people who are different, but who know of Christianity and can therefore be saved.

The *Travels of Sir John Mandeville* presents an ideal of cultural homogeneity. There are four types of people. The first are Mandeville and his readers, the good Christian West. The second, those who are 'strange' and different, but may be turned into participants of the first's culture. The third are Jews, whose difference makes them a threat that must be eliminated. And the fourth, those too different to be considered more than subhuman and who mostly form a monstrous margin beneath all others. It's a concept of culture that today reads like the opening to a dystopian novel, yet it was popular, and as we go on, we'll see the true cost of making worlds like Mandeville's become a reality.

Part III

THE EARLY MODERN AGE

SIMON OF TRENT AND THE CULT OF BLOOD

Things did not improve for Jewish people in medieval Europe in the century that followed the publication of *The Travels of Sir John Mandeville*. Fearmongering and persecution continued to escalate and yet things were about to get even worse – how? The same way so many terrible things begin – with a conspiracy theory. From the mid-twelfth to the thirteenth century, the myth of Jewish blood libel had spread throughout Europe; it was believed that Christians, and particularly Christian children, were being captured and killed by Jews, their blood then used in Jewish religious ceremonies. There didn't need to be evidence or witnesses; if you had a body or a missing child, it was enough. In 1235, thirty-four Jews were killed in the German town of Fulda after the deaths of five children in a house fire, and in a similar case in 1243 in Belitz, near Berlin, the town's entire Jewish population was murdered. These weren't isolated incidents – thousands of Jews were executed all over Europe on the basis of little more than lies and fear. In 1246, Pope Innocent IV added an amendment to the papal bull *Sicut Judaeis* ('As the Jews'), which banned Christians from making claims of blood libel. This did somewhat curtail things for a little while, but it wouldn't take long for the conspiracy to come back, bigger and more brutal than ever before.

On Easter Sunday 1475, the body of a two-year-old boy named Simon was discovered in the city of Trent, in what is now northern Italy. Simon had been missing for a few days and on Good Friday the city's Prince-Bishop, Johannes Hinderbach, oversaw a mass search for the toddler. The focus of the search was, of course, the city's small Jewish population. On the Sunday, a Jewish moneylender called Samuel found Simon's body washed up underneath his house. It appeared the toddler had wandered off and tragically drowned. Samuel and his family immediately alerted the authorities and the search team, at which point Hinderbach got involved once more. In 1475, Passover fell very close to Easter and so Hinderbach quickly concluded that Simon had not drowned, but been kidnapped and murdered so his blood could be used during Passover – the entire Jewish population of Trent was arrested for the crime.

What followed was less a trial and more a wanton avoidance

of justice. When Trent's Jews did not confess to the murder, Hinderbach ordered interrogations under torture. As is often the case with torture confessions, they didn't exactly line up: the methods of murder varied, as did the reasoning behind it and who was involved – but none of that mattered to Hinderbach. He had the evidence he wanted, false or otherwise. In June 1475, Samuel and several other men were burned at the stake for the murder. As for Simon, Hinderbach arranged for the boy's body to be displayed in St Peter's Church, claiming that the child was a martyr. It was said that his body was imbued with the holy spirit and thus could perform miracles. Simon quickly became a lucrative tourist attraction.

By August 1475, Pope Sixtus tried to step in, ordering Hinderbach to stop everything he was doing until papal envoys could be sent to investigate. The envoys arrived in September and Hinderbach immediately raised their suspicions, desperately working to stop them from interviewing the remaining Jewish prisoners, reading trial documents, and even properly examining Simon's body. What they did manage to find was incredibly dark. Alongside the torture, Hinderbach had forged trial documents to speed up guilty verdicts and executions. As for Simon, there were signs on his body that his preservation and cause of death had been falsified. Similarly, the miracles that Hinderbach was profiting from were found to be nothing but a pack of lies. Unsurprisingly, Hinderbach fought back, claiming that the papal envoys had been paid off by a Jewish cabal to cover up the crime. He then further dug his heels in, requesting that Simon be made a saint.

This back and forth continued for several years until 1478. Pope Sixtus managed to release most of Trent's remaining Jewish prisoners, offering them pardon and freedom in return for converting to Christianity. It was a bleak proposal, but after spending years languishing in prison and watching their friends and family die, it was one almost invariably taken up. As for Hinderbach, a papal bull was issued stating that the Trent trials were not illegal, but that the Church disagreed with their conclusion; in addition, the request for Simon to be canonized was refused. This should have been the end of the story, but Hinderbach would not let his cash cow go. In the three years since Simon's death, hundreds of miracles had been attributed to him. Poems and letters and carvings of the toddler were spreading beyond Trent through to Austria and Italy. Hinderbach embraced all of this, commissioning more literature and art and building up a cult-like following around the would-be Saint Simon of Trent.

The impact this cult had in pushing forward their cause was truly catastrophic. In 1493, the martyrdom of Simon was included in the international bestseller *Nuremberg Chronicle*, alongside an illustration of Simon being murdered by a group of visually stereotyped Jews. This picture spread like wildfire around Europe as engravings and in pamphlets. Soon enough, alleged incidences of blood libel were springing up again all over Europe, becoming particularly prevalent in Eastern European countries such as Poland and Lithuania. These cases often came in waves, with notable hot spots in both the fifteenth and sixteenth centuries, and even appearing as late as the early twentieth century. However, the cult of Simon and its accompanying conspiracy never really died out. Perhaps most famously, in May 1934, the 1493 illustration of Simon's death was printed in the German tabloid *Der Stürmer*, as a piece of anti-Semitic Nazi propaganda. When this proved successful in generating fear and hate, the image became a frequent fixture in multiple Nazi and Italian Fascist publications and books, the most insidious use being that of Hellmut Schramm's *Jewish ritual murder, a historical examination* that justified the Nazis' Final Solution.

THE CULT OF SIMON

Today, the cult of Simon marches on and can be found within neo-Nazi and white supremacy groups. In 2019, a gunman entered a San Diego synagogue on the last day of Passover and opened fire, his reason for the hate crime – revenge for Simon of Trent.

THE SPANISH INQUISITION: CORRUPTION AND CONFUSION

To say that nobody expects the Spanish Inquisition is a bit of a misnomer. As we've seen, an ideal of religious and cultural homogeny was becoming popular, as was mass persecution of those that practised Judaism – it was almost inevitable that some kind of widespread authority-led terror was about to happen, and in 1478 two Spanish monarchs stepped up to the plate. The Tribunal of the Holy Office of the Inquisition was set up by Ferdinand II of Aragon and Isabella I of Castile. In 1469, the pair's marriage had effectively unified the separate dominions of Spain, an achievement by any ruler's standard, but Ferdinand and Isabella wanted more. The pair applied to Pope Sixtus IV for a papal bull that would allow them to start an inquisition to root out heresy. This kind of inquisition was not new and had been operated under papal authorities on and off since 1184, but none to the extent that the Spanish Inquisition would manage.

In 1391, anti-Semitism in Spain reached a boiling point when a series of violent pogroms broke out, with places like Aragon, Seville and Valencia seeing mass murders of their Jewish populations. Terrified for their lives, many of Spain's Jews publicly converted to Catholicism. This posed a problem for Ferdinand and Isabella once they came to power. As part of their efforts to unify Spain, they wanted everyone under one religion, Catholicism. But when it came to the new converts – known as *conversos* – it was hard to know who had actually converted and who was just saying they had while secretly practising Judaism. The Inquisition was set up to find out the truth, punish those who had lied about their religion and ensure proper religious conversion.

What were these punishments? Well, contrary to popular belief, executions were actually pretty low down on the punishment roster and there was a very good reason for this. The preferred method was the confiscation of wealth and property. This is arguably better than being burned at the stake; however, it does have two major pitfalls. The first is that the loss of all money and goods rendered a lot of people effectively homeless, which brought in the threat of death anyway, with starvation, exposure and disease exceptionally likely possibilities. The second problem is that confiscation is incredibly susceptible to corruption and this became apparent *very* quickly.

In early 1482, Pope Sixtus IV wrote to the bishops of Spain after receiving a lot of complaints about tribunals making false charges so they could earn a tidy profit: '*In Aragon, Valencia, Mallorca, and Catalonia the Inquisition has for some time been moved not by zeal for the faith and the salvation of souls but by lust for wealth. Many true and faithful Christians, on the testimony of enemies, rivals, slaves, and other lower and even less proper persons, have without any legitimate proof been thrust into secular prisons, tortured and condemned as relapsed heretics, deprived of their goods and property and handed over to the secular arm to be executed, to the peril of souls, setting a pernicious example, and causing disgust to many.*' Sixtus wanted to stop this by having the bishops play a key role in the Inquisition, but Ferdinand II wasn't so keen. Instead, in 1483, he brought in Tomás de Torquemada to become High Inquisitor and oversee the creation of a more regulated inquisition system that would prevent corruption and provide better results.

THE MAN THEY CALLED THE DEVIL

Born in 1420, Tomás de Torquemada came from a religious family, and his mother allegedly converted from Judaism to Catholicism before his birth. He became a Dominican friar and befriended the then Princess Isabella of Castile. It was through this connection that he became entrenched within the royal family, advising on the Inquisition before being chosen to oversee it.

Unfortunately, Torquemada didn't make the system less corrupt, he just made it worse. Under Torquemada, the Inquisition would ride into a town or city and offer an Edict of Grace, a thirty-day period for anyone to confess their sins without the threat of punishment. This time also offered the opportunity to accuse someone else and have this accusation taken seriously. Understandably, this led to a flurry of confessions, both true and false. After all, it was far better to cover your back and confess to something you didn't do and just do penance, than not confess, be falsely accused and face more severe punishment. For those who hadn't confessed but had been accused (or had confessed, just not to the right things), Torquemada recommended torture during interrogations, which in turn led to even more false confessions. More confessions meant more confiscations, which meant even more money. But where did this money go? In a way, the Inquisition worked a little bit like a pyramid scheme. The monarchy and Council of Inquisition were at the top, with a network of local Inquisition tribunals funnelling the wealth upward. Unfortunately, many of the early Inquisition financial documents haven't survived; however, it was reported that Ferdinand and Isabella raked in an alleged 10 million ducats from confiscations.

As the Inquisition escalated, so did fear and mistrust of those outwardly practising Judaism and those known to have converted, which in turn led to a rise in conspiracy theories. One popular notion was that Jews were seizing on the upset to lure converts back to Judaism, while another theory, of course, was blood libel. One such case, dubbed The Holy Child of La Guardia, would prove a major turning point. In late 1491, nine Jewish men and *conversos* were burned at the stake for the kidnap and murder of a child, using the remains in religious rituals. The evidence was scant, as there was no body and no sign that the child had ever actually existed, but the men admitted their guilt under torture. Their confessions helped open the door for the expulsion of Jews from Spain. In early 1492, the Alhambra Decree was issued, declaring that all practising Jews must leave Spain or convert to Catholicism. The exact number of people forced into exile is disputed, though it's often estimated as anywhere between 100,000 and 400,000. Sadly, they would be far from the only religious group persecuted. With the Jews gone, the focus was shifted to Muslims. Following the Spanish conquest and capture of Granada in 1492, Ferdinand and Isabella ended Islamic rule, and shortly after a programme of forced conversions took place. This resulted in a series of riots between 1499 and 1500, with the Muslim population ultimately made to choose between converting to Catholicism or expulsion from their homes and land. However, the persecution didn't end here, and between 1609 and 1614, Spain oversaw the phased forced depopulation of Moriscos (those descended from Muslims who had converted), with around 300,000 people exiled; a sentence that often ended in death, either through starvation, exposure, or simply murder.

The Spanish Inquisition would, in some form, last until 1834. It turned out that persecution paid very well. The fortune amassed through confiscations by Ferdinand and Isabella was just a drop in the bucket. Through later financial documents we can see that confiscation cash ebbed and flowed, but when it hit, it hit pay dirt. For example, in 1678, a spate of mass arrests in Majorca provided a whopping 2.5 million ducats from confiscations. Perhaps this is part of the reason it's now believed that the number of formal executions carried out as a direct result of the Inquisitions was surprisingly low. Modern historians estimating that at the height of these state-officiated deaths, between 1480 and 1530, around 1,000 to 2,000 people were executed, with an estimated 1,000 executions occurring between 1530 and 1826. Corruption and greed had provided a far better option.

MALLEUS MALEFICARUM AND THE INVENTION OF WITCHCRAFT

. . . .

The third and final addition to our canon of books that should never have seen the light of day has had perhaps the most grotesque influence of all, leading to the deaths of tens of thousands of innocent people. The idea of magic and sorcery had long existed throughout most global cultures; indeed, we've already seen mention of it in the tales of Empress Wu and the fall of the Knights Templar. But sorcery wasn't something that was necessarily tied in with the crime of heresy and the devil. This started to shift in the 1300s when the idea of '*learned*' magic hit Western Europe, and clerics began exploring Greek and Arab texts that included alchemy, astrology and spiritual conduct. The Catholic Church wasn't exactly a fan of this new interest in magic, and around 1324 it first started categorizing sorcery as heresy. Interestingly, this appeared in a kind of 'Inquisition for Dummies' manual written by papal inquisitor Bernard Gui, who'd never actually tried a sorcerer and so had to just make up what inquisitors should look for.

Come the 1430s, this fear and fascination had stepped up a level. Whereas Gui had to come up with his sorcerer checklist on the fly, now multiple scholars from across Europe were writing entire books devoted to sorcery and the dangers of magic. The most notable of these was the fifth book in Johannes Nider's series, *Formicarius*. Nider was actually the person who dropped the term 'sorcery' in favour of 'witchcraft' and he directly linked it to demonic practices. To cement his findings, the book even included an interview with an alleged witch from Switzerland – of course, such a juicy read quickly blew up. Still, despite all of this interest and fervour, there still wasn't actually any clear consensus on what witches were or how to stop them. So, although there were some witch trials at this time, there was just so much variation in what people thought about witches that it wasn't widespread – that was all about to change thanks to a man called Heinrich Kramer.

To say that Kramer was somewhat of a sketchy character would be an understatement. A German churchman and papal inquisitor, Kramer had a reputation for lying and stealing, including a 1475 theft charge and a 1482 charge of embezzling war funds, both of which the papacy was kind enough to dust under the rug for him. Kramer's main job was finding religious heretics, but around 1480 he became obsessed with the idea of witchcraft and went somewhat rogue. In the autumn of 1484, he travelled to Ravensburg in southern Germany, where he wasted no time in ardently preaching the dangers of demonic witchcraft. In a matter of days, he was presiding over the trials of eight women, who were found to be witches. As the women burned at the stake, Kramer realized he'd hit something big – witch finding. Unfortunately for him, there was an immediate roadblock – Kramer might have said that killing the eight accused witches was the right thing to do, but there wasn't actually any legal precedent for it and now local officials in Ravensburg were starting to kick up a fuss. Hoping to fix this snag, Kramer journeyed to Rome in the winter of 1484 and requested the papal authority to prosecute witches. Pope Innocent VIII accepted Kramer's plea and issued the papal bull *Summis desiderantes affectibus*, which officially recognized the existence of witches and gave inquisitors the right to prosecute them as they saw fit.

By 1485, Kramer was preparing for his next big witch trial, this time in the Austrian city of Innsbruck. Fourteen people were accused of witchcraft, including a woman called Helena Scheuberin. Kramer and Scheuberin had already crossed paths – upon his arrival in Innsbruck she had urged the community not to attend his sermons and had even suggested that if anyone was a witch, it was Kramer; after all, he was the one obsessed with them. Kramer accused Scheuberin of using witchcraft to commit murder, and as evidence, he delved into her sex life, claiming sexual immorality. This didn't go down well at the trial. The Innsbruck officials were incensed by Kramer using a woman's sexual history as a means to prove witchcraft. This might seem surprising for 1485, especially as women's rights were minimal at best, and for the officials, this really wasn't a question of gender equality, but what counted as heresy. Kramer might say that Scheuberin's sexual history proved heresy, but that was based on his word alone. Kramer was here to find witches, not to punish women based on his own classifications of correct female behaviour and so Scheuberin was acquitted. An infuriated Kramer would not let the ruling lie. Instead, he hung around Innsbruck, collecting (and sometimes fabricating) his own evidence, accosting witnesses, and trying (and failing) to arrest suspects, until eventually in 1486 he was kicked out of the city. Still, Kramer could not let this loss go and so he journeyed to Cologne to write his magnum opus.

TOIL AND TROUBLE

Though it is perhaps the most known witch trial today, the Salem witch trials actually had one of the lowest execution rates, with nineteen people found guilty and hanged between 1692 and 1693. In the seventeenth century, what is now Germany saw its own spate of mass trials, including in Fulda, where an estimated 250 people died; Würzburg, which saw 157 confirmed executions and an estimated 900 deaths across the entire Prince-Bishopric; and Bamburg, where 900 lost their lives between 1626 and 1632.

Published in 1487, *Malleus Maleficarum* is split into three sections:

1. Why witches are real and joined to the devil.
2. How witches practise dangerous magic.
3. What inquisitors can do to catch a witch, gain their confession and, crucially, execute them.

Kramer borrowed much of the book's information from the 1430s witch scholar boom, including great chunks of Nider's *Formicarius*. Alongside this, Kramer and his inquisitor colleague Jacob Sprenger delved into the world of myth and folklore, pulling out traditional stories and bending them into their classification of witches. One example of this was the *Bonae Res*, thirteenth-century tales of women who could fly, pass through locked doors and often left friendly gifts of food on tables – now Kramer's witches could fly and pass through locked doors (though they didn't leave gifts, as that's not exceptionally demonic). Bolstering these claims were Kramer's personal accounts of witchcraft, most of which were likely fabricated as there are few indicators he was involved in any witchcraft trials earlier than 1484. Unsurprisingly given Kramer's humiliation in Innsbruck, *Malleus Maleficarum* also details how women, as the weaker sex, are far more likely to be witches than men. The most common candidate for witchcraft was an outspoken woman, one with a bad reputation, a high sex drive, or rumoured sex life beyond the boundaries of marriage. Concrete evidence wasn't needed to bring charges; a rumour was enough, and when confessions were not forthcoming, Kramer advocated torture or lying to the condemned as means of extraction.

The book was a runaway hit. There had been treatises on witches before, but none had a papal bull (*Summis desiderantes affectibus*) tacked to the front. Kramer made it clear that witchcraft was a great, if not the greatest, threat to the Church, religion and all good Christian people. This call to arms was taken up across Europe, and from the book's publication until the late seventeenth century, a witch-hunting frenzy took hold. The *Malleus Maleficarum* was the witch-hunters' bible, but Kramer's classifications for witches would be built on over time, with additions such as witches' marks thrown in for good measure. In total, an estimated 50,000 people, mainly women, were killed. All of this hysteria and death, because of one man and his inability to let a failure go.

THE SAGA OF POPE JOAN

Said to have reigned in Rome during the Middle Ages, Pope Joan has been called everything from a 'Catholic cover-up' to a forgotten feminist martyr. The tale of her short reign as pope between 855 and 857 fascinated medieval audiences and almost helped bring the Catholic Church to its knees during the Reformation – but was Pope Joan even real to begin with?

The origins of Pope Joan's existence are littered with what can best be described as historical red flags. The first mention of her comes from 1255, centuries after her supposed lifetime.

Dominican Jean de Mailly writes of a pope who was discovered to be a woman when she began giving birth on the street, the crowd quickly turning and stoning her to death. Within the next twenty years, two more major accounts appeared, each differing from the other. The first was that of Dominican Étienne de Bourbon, who states that the *'astonishing stroke of audacity or rather of insanity'* happened in 1100. However, between 1265 and 1277, Dominican Martinus Polonus moved the story back to around 855, in his chronicles on Roman popes and emperors. It's actually Polonus's version that became the most popular and built on – an Englishwoman born in Mainz, Joan, and her lover, went to Athens, where she lived as a man called John. Known for her unparalleled intelligence, Joan was unanimously elected as pope, a position she held for *'two years, seven months and four days'*. During a procession, Joan went into labour and gave birth *'in a narrow passage between the Coliseum and San Clement'*, dying shortly after. Polonus explains that there are no papal records of Joan, *'on account of the deformity of the female sex'*.

As we've already seen, when historical accounts appear out of the blue centuries after the fact, their validity is often dubious. Suspicions are raised even further when those accounts change so drastically with each retelling that things become less based on historical facts and more an experiment of the scholarly rumour mill. This is very much the case for Pope Joan. Beyond these early accounts, there really isn't much evidence that she ever existed, and the evidence being offered by Mailly, Bourbon and Polonus is flimsy at best. Yet sometimes in history, it doesn't

matter if a story is a lie if that story is entertaining and so the myth of Pope Joan became fact.

Much like when Geoffrey of Monmouth's Arthurian legend gained a seat at the historical table, the ripple effects at first were not that big. Arguably, beyond being embarrassing for the Catholic Church, the only notable blow was a medieval rumour that, thanks to Pope Joan's deception, all newly elected popes had to sit on a special chair with a key-shaped hole so that their genitalia could be checked. Funnily enough, this chair actually did exist, but the hole was representative of a commode – the new pope rising from the chair as a kind of metaphor for humble beginnings and to show that even the pope was human. Yet, as the years progressed the legend of Joan progressed beyond schoolyard tales of genital chairs and became a very real threat to the Catholic Church.

Fourteenth-century religious reformer Jan Hus was one of the first to use Joan to lobby against papal supremacy.

He argued that Joan's time as pope showed that either God didn't actually ordain each pope or that the Church had knowingly operated without a divinely ordered leader. Hus's stand against the Church ultimately ended with his execution in 1415; however, his ideas about Pope Joan didn't die with him. At the time, nobody believed a woman could legitimately rule as pope, much less a woman famed for having a lover, giving birth out of wedlock, and disguising herself as a man. So, if Pope Joan was real, she encompassed massive flaws in the operation of the Catholic Church. If she wasn't real – well, that didn't actually matter, as the Church had never said she wasn't. Thus, she was the perfect stick to beat them with.

During the sixteenth century, the Catholic Church faced major criticism from religious reformers who questioned the Church's teachings as well as incidences of its corruption and abuses of power. Pope Joan became the embodiment of everything reformers found wrong with the Church, and the arguments of Jan Hus were their focal point. However, as with everything Pope Joan, people couldn't help but build on her story. Mentions of her intellectual brilliance were removed and instead much was made of supposed sexual immorality – and in turn, that of the Church. Playwright John Bale claimed it was Joan's chaplain's child she gave birth to, and the Bishop of Salisbury argued in 1560 that Joan must be given a place in papal history as she was just as sexually depraved as other peers such as John XIII who had allegedly committed incest. Soon things went even further, with several reformers such as

FAKE ARTEFACTS FOR A FAKE POPE

As the myth became popularized, many forged artefacts claiming to prove Joan's existence began to appear, including coins, busts and other relics. This has all helped keep the legend alive, and to this day some historians and archaeologists have continued to seek to demonstrate that the female pope was real – unfortunately, so far none have been successful.

Pier Paolo Vergerio claiming Joan was actually a necromancer and witch, the devil securing her rise to popehood.

As the reformer rumour mill spun ever further out of control, Roman Catholic authors made attempts to prove that Joan had never been real, but nothing really stuck. Finally, in 1601, Pope Clement VIII declared the existence of Pope Joan to be untrue. Still, reformers continued to utilize Pope Joan in their fight against the Church. The Protestant Reformation would ultimately win out and cause the split between what is now the Roman Catholic Church and Protestantism. It wouldn't be until the seventeenth century that Pope Joan was proved to be a myth, ironically by a Protestant historian, David Blondel.

PERKIN WARBECK: THE GREAT PRETENDER

. . . .

Between 1455 and 1485, England had been ensnared in a series of bloody civil wars, known as the Wars of the Roses. The incompetent reign of Henry VI had resulted in losses of land and wealth, while corruption festered within the king's court. In 1454, Henry succumbed to a sudden psychosis that left him catatonic and barely able to function let alone rule. This led to a power grab over the role of Lord Protector, passing back and forth between rival factions of the royal House of Plantagenet via a veritable cavalcade of schemes and plots. Ultimately, an all-out war broke out, between the Houses of York (the White Rose) and Lancaster (the Red Rose).

A conclusion to this now decades-long battle began to emerge in 1483 when Edward IV died. The crown went to his son Edward V, who at just twelve years old was too young to rule, with Edward IV's brother Richard becoming Lord Protector until the boy king came of age. However, Richard sought the throne for himself and had Edward, along with his eight-year-old brother, Richard of Shrewsbury, Duke of York, held in the Tower of London. The now infamous Richard III was crowned in July 1483 and the little princes mysteriously vanished – almost certainly killed. Unsurprisingly, most people were not overjoyed at Richard's route to the throne and his right to rule was tenuous at best. Lancastrian Henry Tudor took this as an opportunity to stake his own claim to the throne. In August 1485, the two sides met once more at the Battle of Bosworth. Richard III was defeated and killed, leaving Henry Tudor the new King of England. Yet just over a decade later, his rule was questioned by a pretender named Perkin Warbeck.

LAMBERT SIMNEL

Warbeck was the second major pretender threat to Henry VII, the first being Lambert Simnel, a young boy who was presented as first Richard, Duke of York, and then Edward of Warwick. Simnel was at the heart of a Yorkist attempt to overthrow the new king in 1487. The attempt failed and Simnel became a kitchen boy in the king's court.

Not much is known about the early life of Perkin Warbeck. He was born around 1474 to a poor family in Flanders, and would later move to work as a servant and apprentice in Antwerp. Around 1491, his work led him to Cork, Ireland, and it was there that people started to notice that if you squinted, Perkin Warbeck had a bit of a Plantagenet look about him. The exact reasoning for why Warbeck began to claim to be an heir to the English throne is murky; however, he first purported to be Edward Plantagenet, 17th Earl of Warwick, the son of George Plantagenet, brother to Edward IV and Richard III.

Unfortunately, this would have been very difficult as Warwick was currently a prisoner in the Tower of London, where he'd been held since 1485. So, Warbeck changed his claim, and he was now the youngest lost prince, Richard of York. According to him, his older brother Edward had indeed been murdered, but he was spared thanks to his youth and innocence. Since then, he'd lived in secrecy in Europe, but now he was back and ready to claim the English throne.

Warbeck's story was incredibly silly to say the least. Aside from the initial flip-flopping claims of who he was, he was still learning to speak English, which was a bit suspicious considering that, if his tale was to be believed, he'd left England when he was nine. Still, for those looking to take down the Tudors, Warbeck and his story were useful if nothing else. Over the next few years, Warbeck was sent around the great European courts and was accepted as Richard of York by Charles VIII of France and the Holy Roman Emperor, Maximilian I. Even Margaret of Burgundy, the sister of Edward IV, claimed Warbeck as her nephew, though this was likely less because she believed him, and more because she wanted her family's throne back, not to mention that Henry Tudor had killed her husband.

In July 1495, with the help of Margaret of Burgundy, Warbeck set forth to win his crown. However, when he landed in the English town of Deal, he was met with strong resistance from local forces loyal to Tudor King Henry VII. Warbeck swiftly fled to Ireland, where his forces attempted to invade Waterford and failed once more. Tail between his legs, Warbeck ran to Scotland, where he was granted refuge by King James IV. Just like the King

of France, James IV likely didn't believe Warbeck's story, but it made him an excellent pawn in undermining the new Tudor rule and attempting to win English land. In September 1496, with Scottish support, yet another invasion of England went ahead, and again it was a huge failure. The Scottish troops just used it as a border invasion, while the Yorkist supporters Warbeck had been depending on to rise up on his account never showed up. But the key to a final push for the crown appeared in 1497. In June that year, Cornwall had seen a rebellion against the Crown in response to Henry VII raising taxes. Seemingly keen to get rid of the failure that was Perkin Warbeck, and make him someone else's problem, James IV urged Warbeck to join the Cornish uprising and form his own army. In September, he arrived on the Cornish coast and managed to raise a force several thousand strong. However, most of Warbeck's new army weren't carrying weapons, and so when the king's forces met them it was all over.

Henry VII was harsh on the Cornish rebels and executed their leaders, but he chose to spare Perkin Warbeck. By now Warbeck had admitted that he wasn't Richard of York, just some guy from Flanders, and so Henry VII held him at his own court. Warbeck was a prisoner, but he wasn't in a cell and he wasn't facing death; in fact, within the court he had relative freedom – as prisons went, this was very comfortable. Still, in 1498, Warbeck attempted to escape and was immediately sent to the Tower of London. It was there that he met Warwick, the man he'd initially pretended to be. This was not good for Warwick – the last surviving male Plantagenet heir, he'd been a prisoner in the Tower since he was ten, and in the thirteen years that had passed, he'd lived quietly, perhaps due to the fact that allegedly such early confinement had led to Warwick losing his grip on reality. Yet Warbeck had proved that any Plantagenet heir, real or fake, was a threat that couldn't be contained. In early 1499, another Warwick pretender appeared and although they were swiftly crushed, Henry VII decided enough was enough. A likely fabricated plot was suddenly uncovered, in which Warbeck and Warwick would escape the Tower. His excuse in place, Henry Tudor ordered the deaths of both men, and in November 1499 they were executed. The Plantagenet threat was dead, and the Tudor reign cemented.

THE DONATION OF CONSTANTINE

As we've seen, the fifteenth century was packed with moments that would spark centuries-long movements: the Spanish Inquisition, the European witch craze and blood libel hysteria.

But there was another moment, another lie, that although at first quieter, would prove just as explosive.

Born in 1406, Italian scholar Lorenzo Valla is quite unlike anyone we've met so far. Valla was fascinated with the idea of truth and the role that rhetoric plays in how we as individuals understand fact and fiction. In 1439, he wrote a book, *Dialectical Disputations*, in which he argued that truth doesn't necessarily come from events or facts, but from what is presented to us, a kind of proposal of truth that we can pick and choose from. For example, we know that the *Malleus Maleficarum* isn't true; it's a lucky dip of folklore, medieval academia and the random thoughts of Heinrich Kramer. But we can believe it is true – that the world around us is often full of unknowns and that the logic Kramer provides fills in those gaps. And if we understand it to be true, then, for us, it is true. This was an incredibly modern idea, especially for the 1400s, and predictably, it didn't really earn Valla any friends – especially within the Church. In fact, it earned him a reputation of being both a professional heretic and what we'd now call a troll. His work was so inflammatory and brought so many questions to the Church's door that, surely, he had to be doing it for attention – some scholars just want to watch the world burn. It's likely that it was this view of Valla and his work that would lead to his most important find being falsely debunked.

In 1440, Valla was working for Alfonso V of Aragon, King of Naples. Alfonso was in a heated dispute with Pope Eugene IV over the papal state's claims on his kingdom, specifically Naples. Eugene was adamant that the papacy had rights to

Alfonso's lands thanks to a fourth-century decree known as *The Donation of Constantine*. According to the papacy, Emperor Constantine I had given the entirety of the western part of the Roman Empire over to them, as thanks for Pope Sylvester I miraculously curing him of leprosy. Interestingly, the Church wouldn't actually act on Constantine's supposed gift for several centuries, but once they did, they went all-in on it. The decree was extremely useful in consolidating power, ensuring the Church had control over countries' ecclesiastic elite, and of course, seizing and maintaining land. In Alfonso's mind, *The Donation of Constantine* was too good to be true and so he tasked Lorenzo Valla with investigating his suspicions.

It didn't take long for Valla to find that the decree was a fake – an eighth-century forgery. Valla found that the language used in the document didn't match up with fourth-century dialect, noting that there were so many inaccuracies that the papacy had to know it was a fake, likely because they'd done the forgery themselves. Valla put his findings into a manuscript, *Discourse on the Alleged Donation of Constantine*, and he was far from subtle in laying out his allegations: '*For during some centuries now, either they have not known that the* Donation of Constantine *is spurious and forged, or else they themselves forged it, and their successors walking in the same way of deceit as their elders have defended as true … confounding everything with murders, disasters and crimes. They say the city of Rome is theirs, theirs the kingdom of Sicily and of Naples, the whole of Italy, the Gauls, the Spains, the Germans, the Britons, indeed the whole West; for all these are contained in the instrument of the Donation itself.'* Yet before Valla's work could even get out of the gate, the Church debunked it – this was Lorenzo Valla after all – he was just after attention, yet again.

Seventy-seven years later, in 1517, Valla's manuscript was finally published, and in the years that followed it would be read by some of the most important European figures of the day. Arguably, its most influential reader was German priest and theologian Martin Luther, who picked up Valla's work in 1520. Three years earlier, Luther had set in motion what would become known as the Protestant Reformation (or European Reformation) with his publication of *Ninety-five Theses*. This was a long list of issues with the Catholic Church, including the ability for people to buy their way out of punishment for sins after death, by giving money to the Church. When Luther

FATHER OF THE REFORMATION

One of the most influential figures of the sixteenth century, Martin Luther became a monk in 1505 after he was almost struck by lightning. His criticisms of the Church would push forward the Reformation and the development of the Protestant religion. However, in his later years, he would write rhetoric against Jewish people, which would go on to feed anti-Semitic ideology, some of which can be found as late as the Third Reich.

read Valla's work, he saw it as yet another sign that the Catholic Church was becoming too corrupt to operate, making up its own truths to cash in and hold power, writing: '*The Donation of Constantine is a forgery. Good heavens! What a darkness and wickedness is at Rome! You wonder at the judgement of God that such unauthentic, crass, impudent lies not only lived but prevailed for so many centuries!*' In 1521, the Church excommunicated Luther and went on to declare him a heretic, but unlike Valla, his voice could not be easily suppressed. Thanks to the invention of the printing press, Luther's works calling out the Church for corruption and deceit could be read like never before. His pamphlets and books could be found in towns and cities across Europe, opening the floodgates for new ideas on religion and criticism of the once all-powerful Catholic Church. The European Reformation had begun.

THE AZTEC CONQUEST

In the sixteenth century, as the Reformation rolled on, Spain became something of a byword for cruelty, atrocity and oppression. They were the villains of Europe and the world at large. The idea that they were religious fanatics, who'd proved their brutality during the Inquisition, was first prominently popularized by the 1567 book *Sanctae Inquisitionis Hispanicae Artes* (*Exposition of the Arts of the Spanish Holy Inquisition*). The book contained an illustration that depicted how thousands upon thousands of people were tortured and executed during the Inquisition. Now, this was a fallacy – as we know, although a large number of people were executed during the Inquisition, the actual figures were far lower than those that were now to become popularized. Added to this was that in the hysteria focused on overexaggerated mass burnings, the knowledge of the expulsion of Jews and Muslims from Spain became lost. After all, stories of bloody executions of innocents are far more immediately lurid than the systematic oppression and expulsion of religious groups. And this became the fixed narrative of the Spanish Inquisition, one that wasn't so much true but left the reader more easily horrified by its visceral nature, without having to delve into the complexities of corruption, greed and racism.

This birthed what would become known in the twentieth century as the Black Legend – a falsified version of the darker aspects of Spanish history. This spinning of historic facts would soon move beyond the Inquisition and Reformation, to include colonial atrocities, particularly those around the Spanish conquest of the Aztec Empire. This is the most popular narrative of the conquest that you'll find in many history textbooks: in 1519, several hundred Spanish conquistadors, led by Hernán Cortés, arrived in the Aztec capital of Tenochtitlán. In November, Cortés met with Emperor Moctezuma, who, believing the conquistadors to be gods, essentially handed over his empire and was swiftly placed under house arrest. Though the Aztecs revolted, they were quickly quashed by the might of the Europeans, who seized their wealth and land, killing them both by the blade and through unintended germ warfare – smallpox. By 13 August 1521, Tenochtitlán had fallen into Spanish hands – the conquest a success.

TENOCHTITLÁN

The capital of the Aztec Empire, Tenochtitlán was founded around 1325. Split symmetrically into four quadrants, surrounding a centre, it was one of the most magnificent cities in the world. The conquistadors even struggled to put into words how great its architecture and cultural marvels were. The city is estimated to have been home to 200,000 to 400,000 people.

As historians Matthew Restall and Camilla Townsend have argued, this popularized account is based far more on myth than it is fact. It was partially warped by the fifteenth and sixteenth centuries' fixation on the Black Legend and that Spain was always up to something terrible, but was also tarnished by European opinions on culture and societies outside themselves, which stripped back the parts of the Aztecs that were deemed too other to possibly understand. Much like the Inquisition, a more simplistic story was created. The villains – Spain – massacred an entire empire and the victims – the Aztecs – were far too indigenous and ill-equipped to fight back against such a

European power. This take has created a substantial amount of damage to our shared historic knowledge.

Before we delve into the true history, it's good to get an idea of just how deep this hole of misinformation goes. One great example is popular knowledge concerning the Aztecs' practice of human sacrifice, much of which has unravelled in two different but equally incorrect ways. The first reports on the Aztec use of sacrifice came from Spain following the conquest, and as such many historians saw them as overexaggerations designed to justify Spain's actions. The other angle took these reports as facts, but disregarded much of the Aztec cultural significance around religion and gift offering, instead creating an inflated and often fabricated notion of rampant bloody barbarism. Fortunately, recent archaeological digs of the remains of Tenochtitlán below Mexico City are changing this narrative. In 1521, conquistador Andrés de Tapia described seeing a tower formed of sacrificed skulls near one of the city's main temples, Templo Mayor, which was designed to spark fear into enemies. This was brushed off as Spanish propaganda; however, in 2017, the tower was unearthed, consisting of about 650 skulls. Further archaeological work at Tenochtitlán has revealed multiple other displays of sacrifice, notable for including not only the remains of sacrificed men and captured warriors but of women and children – something that surprised the archaeological team as historically they weren't thought to be a part of such military focused sacrifice. So, the Spanish weren't lying and we still don't know everything about how the Aztec Empire operated – between the myth and the truth of the Aztec conquest there is still so much left to discover,

but there are some factors we definitely know and they go against almost everything in the popular account.

When Cortés and Moctezuma met in early November 1519, the emperor did not hand over his rule. Instead, he governed for at least several more weeks, if not months. Moctezuma was well aware of Cortés and his conquistadors – since they'd landed in Mexico he'd been keeping an eye on them. Before arriving at Tenochtitlán, Cortés and his men had spent the last few months attacking people, trying to form alliances, forcing conversions, enslaving, and committing the odd massacre. None of the groups the Spaniards had come across mistook them for a god – maniacs, probably, but not gods. In September 1519, Cortés formed an alliance with the Nahua state Tlaxcala, which had been engaged in an intermittent war, the Flower Wars, with the Aztec Empire for decades. Indeed, it was alongside the Tlaxcalans that Cortés met Moctezuma in November. By this point, Moctezuma had spent months trying to work out the best course of action. He didn't want a war and so he welcomed the Spaniards to gain more intel on them. Relations remained tense until April 1520, when Moctezuma was told that a fleet of Spanish ships was headed towards Tenochtitlán. But the ships weren't there to invade; they were there for Cortés.

In 1518, the Spanish governor of Cuba, Diego Velázquez, had given Cortés permission for an expedition to Mexico; however, this was quickly retracted. So, when Cortés landed in Mexico in 1519, he was doing so without Spanish permission. Now, in April 1520, Velázquez had sent a fleet under the command of Pánfilo de Narváez, to find and stop the rogue Cortés. On hearing of the fleet, Moctezuma told his people to prepare for war, but Cortés – aware that the jig was up and two rival groups of Spaniards were about to collide – impulsively took Moctezuma hostage, keeping him as his prisoner. He hoped this would show Narváez that he was in control of the Aztec Empire and win his allegiance. In May, Cortés left Tenochtitlán to travel to where Narváez and his men were in Cempoala; there he swiftly defeated Narváez – the rival force either joining Cortés or being taken prisoner. However, in his absence, Cortés's second in command, Pedro de Alvarado, had caused an uprising in Tenochtitlán. During celebrations for the festival Tōxcatl, the Spaniards had massacred the nobles and warriors inside the city's Great Temple. Realizing that the entire city had now turned against them, the Spanish and remaining Tlaxcalans walled themselves up in their fortress, while the Mexica besieged them from outside.

Imprisoned though he was, Moctezuma knew that more foreign forces were coming, too many for his people to withstand without major loss of life. It was the job of any Nahua leader, be they chief or emperor, to put the lives of their people first, so they could continue. And so, Moctezuma declared to the Mexica fighting: *'we are not their match.'* It was this that would later be taken out of context and often moved further forward in the timeline, to show Moctezuma as giving up on the empire. Yet, the fighting did continue, Moctezuma was killed, and ultimately the Spanish fled. It looked like Tenochtitlán had been saved, but really Cortés was just in Tlaxcala regrouping. Much like he had with the Tlaxcalans, Cortés worked on building alliances with areas under Mexica rule, both through promises of rewards and the threat that if you didn't join the Spanish side, Cortés might raid your land and murder you. During this coalition quest, smallpox was sweeping through Mexico Valley and Tenochtitlán, likely brought into the country by one of Narváez's men. The Mexica had never experienced the disease and had no way of fighting it – soon it had killed many.

Come May 1521, Cortés was ready to fight once more. The Mexica had been crippled by smallpox and had lost an estimated 30 to 50 per cent of the population. However, the Spanish forces had grown substantially, thanks to its alliances. Indeed, Matthew Restall argues that so changed was Cortés's force that in the unfolding Siege of Tenochtitlán, it's likely that at times less than 1 per cent of the invading force was Spanish. The siege itself lasted from May to August and was a constant back and forth of victory and losses. Considering that the Mexica were still recovering from smallpox, had their food lines cut off, and were now grappling with a dysentery outbreak, they held out for an astounding amount of time. However, by 13 August, they could fight no more and surrendered. Tenochtitlán was now in Cortés's hands.

In the coming years, it was Cortés that spun the myth of how he beat the Aztecs, how they saw him as a god, and were no match for his might. This couldn't be further from the truth. There is little about Cortés's conquest that is impressive, and arguably, much of his success was down to luck. However, his lies, intermingled with the mythology of the Black Legend, irrecoverably changed the historical narrative into one unrecognizable from actual events.

HENRY VIII AND TURNING A LIE INTO LAW

As Luther's ideas for a reformed Church spread, things really started to heat up in Europe. In 1524, a series of revolts broke out in German-speaking European countries. This would become known as the German Peasants' War. As the violence reached its apex in 1525, leaders of the rebellions released their list of demands, which included multiple Reformation ideals, such as the ability to elect preachers, to be preached to in an understandable way, and for barriers to be put in place to prevent unnecessary funds being funnelled away from the community and to the Catholic Church. There were of course other demands – freedom from serfdom, reduced compulsory labour, and return of land seized by the nobility – however, it was the ones that condemned the actions of the Catholic Church that sparked fear and rage; the Reformation threat had spiralled so far out of control that now *even* peasants, the lowest of the low, had taken up its banner. Martin Luther quickly jumped ship, publishing *Against the Murderous, Thieving Hordes of Peasants*, which likened the rebels to '*the devil's own*' and urged swift and bloody punishment. This was deftly dealt out, the peasants quashed, their rights taken away and an estimated 100,000 dead by the rebellion's end. Yet it wasn't only the peasants who'd lost; the wheels of reformation slowed almost to a stop. Those outside the nobility were left with a bad taste in their mouths, following Luther pushing the German rebels under the bus. As for Europe's elite, they dug their heels in, afraid of what other violence might spring up. It looked like the Reformation might be dead in the water, or at least in need of a long rehabilitation. That was until England took up the mantle.

Ironically, England's King Henry VIII was a staunch Catholic and in 1522 had even been given the title of 'Defender of the Faith' by the papacy after speaking out against Martin Luther. However, this all changed when Henry decided he wanted to divorce his wife, Catherine of Aragon. Catherine had not provided him with a male heir and, more pressingly, Henry really wanted to get together with Catherine's lady-in-waiting, Anne Boleyn, who had made it clear that she would only be his wife, not his mistress. In 1527, Henry wrote to Pope

Clement VII requesting a divorce. This was turned down, and a back and forth continued until, eventually, Clement told Henry in no uncertain terms that the divorce was not happening and if he remarried, he'd be excommunicated. Luckily, Henry's right-hand man, Thomas Cromwell, had a plan B. Cromwell wasn't wholly on board with all of Martin Luther's ideology, but he did have Reformation leanings, having read the likes of Lorenzo Valla, and he believed that for Christianity to function, it needed reforms that the Catholic Church couldn't and wouldn't provide. So he suggested that England break away from the Church. This would procure Henry his much sought for divorce and lead England towards reformation. The plan worked – the marriage to Catherine of Aragon was declared invalid, Henry and Anne Boleyn wed, and in 1534 the Act of Supremacy was passed, naming Henry VIII supreme head of the Church of England.

Cutting the cord with the Catholic Church involved a lot of paperwork. For one thing, England had to establish new rules and laws to replace those that had once gone through the papacy, as well as consolidate power by moving crimes that had previously been tried in ecclesiastical courts to the state and civil courts. One such crime was Buggery, here meaning anal intercourse with men, women and animals. In 1533, the Buggery Act was passed, declaring it a crime punishable by death, with the act due to last until the end of the next parliament, when it would be reviewed again. Interestingly, the creator of the act, Thomas Cromwell, does not appear to have intended the act to target homosexuality, instead using it as a legal loophole under which members of the Catholic Clergy, such as monks and priests, could be executed. The Buggery Act was not necessarily intended to be enforced but to weaken the power of the Catholic Church and pose a threat to its clergy. With that job done it was consigned to effective oblivion, a forgotten law that would never actually be used – at least that was the plan.

Dull paperwork aside, perhaps the biggest issue that came out of the break from the Catholic Church was Henry VIII himself. Henry was already fast gaining a reputation as someone who would do whatever they needed to get their own way – now this tyrant had just been handed even more autonomy and the ability to face very few consequences for his actions. It could only end well.

In 1536, Henry signed the death warrant for his second wife, Anne Boleyn. Once the woman he wanted to risk it all for, Henry had grown tired of her and set his sights on a new flame

(Anne's lady-in-waiting, Jane Seymour). Wanting Anne out of the picture, he fabricated a series of crimes, including adultery, incest and witchcraft, which duly saw Anne beheaded. Fast forward to 1540 and Henry was on to his fourth wife, Anne of Cleves, and in a predictable turn of events, he now wanted her gone so he could wed her lady-in-waiting, Catherine Howard. The problem was that the marriage to Anne of Cleves had been put in place by Thomas Cromwell as a strategic political move to help England's Reformation. By marrying into the Germanic House of Cleves, Henry would gain a Protestant ally, which would help fend off European Catholic powers Spain and France, as well as hopefully quelling unrest at the religious change within England. Nonetheless, Henry had Anne agree to an annulment.

This left Cromwell on shaky ground. Henry wasn't happy he'd had to marry Anne in the first place, and several uprisings such as 1536's Pilgrimage of Grace, had shown that Cromwell's route to Reformation wasn't wholly plain sailing for the megalomaniac monarch. Taking advantage of the situation, Cromwell's enemies at court started a rumour that Cromwell was plotting treason against the king, and his fate was sealed – in June 1540, Cromwell was sentenced to death.

But Henry VIII was not happy with just beheading his former favourite, he sought to blacken Cromwell's name. To do this, the king planned to have Cromwell executed alongside the most despicable nobleman possible – Walter Hungerford. It was known that Hungerford imprisoned and tortured his wife, Elizabeth, starving her and allegedly trying to kill her.

In fact, Cromwell had ignored Elizabeth's pleas for a divorce. Yet, much like Cromwell, Henry and his council overlooked Elizabeth's plight when it came to creating charges against Hungerford, instead charging him with treason for employing a Pilgrimage of Grace supporter. With the key treason charge in place, Henry was free to fabricate two additional charges. The first was for using magic and the second was buggery. Henry would use Cromwell's own act against him, eliminating its original purpose for the sake of humiliation.

RELIGIOUS REBELS

The Pilgrimage of Grace was a major rebellion that threatened the power of Henry VIII. Led by Robert Aske, it protested against the break from the Catholic Church and the Dissolution of the Monasteries. For a time, it looked like it might jeopardize the Tudor reign. However, the pilgrims were promised a diplomatic agreement to end their protest. This would turn out to be a lie – Aske and 200 others were executed and Henry VIII continued his break from Rome.

On 28 July 1540, Walter Hungerford became the first person to be convicted and executed under the Buggery Act. To ensure the execution went through, an amendment was passed that made the 1533 Act *observed and kept for ever*. Interestingly, forever proved to be a tenuous thing and the Act was briefly repealed in 1553. However, it was quickly brought back in 1562, with the wording added by Henry VIII in 1540 loud and clear; this time forever would be *'forever'*.

And so it has been. In England, thousands of men were charged under the Act and hundreds were executed before it was finally replaced in 1828 with the Offences Against the Person Act. Yet the Buggery Act lived on; as part of British colonization, the act was sewn into multiple countries' laws, where, in some places, it remains to this day. The Buggery Act thus remains perhaps one of history's most horrific examples of the ripple effect.

THE MANY (MANY) LIES
OF NOSTRADAMUS

It's rare for an over 450-year-old book to make headline news today, but that is the magic and mysticism of Nostradamus. In 2020, it was widely reported in newspapers across the world that Michel de Nostredame's 1555 *Les Prophéties* had predicted the global pandemic that was Covid-19. This wasn't a new phenomenon: in recent years, Nostredame (or Nostradamus) has been said to have foreseen everything from 9/11 to 2012, aka the end of the world that never was. Even before that, Nostradamus's prophecies have been linked to the Great Fire of London (1666), the Treaty of Hamedan (1727) and the French Revolution. Now it would be very easy to write all of this off as a centuries-old hoax – the 2020 Covid prediction certainly was, not actually coming from *Les Prophéties*, but from someone who was likely very bored on the internet one day. Yet that is what makes Nostradamus so fascinating. His prophecies are so vague they could mean anything and can be imitated by anyone. It's what's made them endure for centuries, but it's also what makes them so dangerous.

Born in 1503, Nostradamus began his career in prophecies around 1550. After years of travelling around France, Nostradamus settled in Salon-de-Provence in southern France, where he worked primarily as a physician, particularly renowned for his treatment of plague victims. This was a profitable line of work, but very dependent on waves of sickness, so to make up his income Nostradamus began to dabble in other areas. First came a series of recipes for his patients, which included teeth-whitening powders, hair dyes and even love potions. Off the back of this success, he moved into astrology, promising his clientele medical treatment that went beyond the care of the body, including insight into the mind and future, creating individual detailed horoscopes. These horoscopes tended to lean towards more favourable futures for his customers, though when he did predict a dark path ahead, he would often couch it in reminders that for a life to be well lived it must contain both peaks and valleys.

In 1550, Nostradamus seized upon a new idea, publishing. The book trade was flourishing and publishers were especially keen on printing almanacs, annual works that could be anything from a doctor listing the best times of year to bleed

PLAGUE DOCTORING

Despite Nostradamus's reputation as a great healer of plague victims, his techniques weren't actually that useful. For example, he used bloodletting, which was one of the oldest medical practices and can be found in Ancient Egypt and Greece, as well as a treatment during the Black Death. Indeed, bloodletting remained popular through to the 1800s; however, it does very little, especially if you're already fighting a disease, in which case it increases your chances of infection and anaemia and of course, accidentally draining too much blood.

oneself to crop-harvesting manuals. Nostradamus jumped on this, expanding from individual horoscopes to broad annual tellings of the future. On top of everything else he was, Nostradamus also saw himself as a poet, choosing to write most of his predictions in four-line verses known as quatrains. This gave his prophecies an almost mystical feel but also offered a sense of vaguery – they could mean anything to anyone, so it was up to the reader to interpret them. These annual almanacs almost immediately took off and soon Nostradamus had a burgeoning following. In 1555, he added the Queen of France, Catherine de' Medici, to his growing clientele and, through her patronage, began providing predictions to her husband, King Henry II. That same year, Nostradamus published a compendium of his predictions, *Les Prophéties*. But it would take something far bigger to cement Nostradamus's reputation.

In 1559, Henry II died following a jousting tournament, when a lance carried by Gabriel Montgomery splintered around his eye causing brain damage and eventually sepsis. The death shocked France, as nobody could have foreseen the forty-year-old king dying in such a freak accident. But then people remembered Nostradamus's 1559 Almanac, which cited '*the great one to be no more*'. Popularity then surged around another prediction: '*The young lion shall overcome the old, on the field of battle in a single duel he'll put his eyes in his cage of gold, winner taking all, then a death most cruel.*' – Henry was wearing a gilded helmet when his eye was pierced, the old lion falling to the younger Montgomery. Nostradamus had known this would happen all along. A feverish fascination began, dissecting *Les Prophéties* for warnings and signs that may have been missed. This all ignored that in 1558 Nostradamus declared Henry II '*invincible*'.

In 1566, Nostradamus died, yet his prophecies never stopped coming, thanks to a series of fakes and forgeries. Some were fairly obvious, other astrologists slapping the name 'Nostradamus' onto their works to boost sales, or publishers printing counterfeit editions of *Les Prophéties* with supposedly new prophecies to entice readers. A parade of false relatives soon appeared including one who claimed to be Nostradamus's son and actually managed to land a publishing deal with Nostradamus's own publisher. Stranger still was the story spun by French doctor and flour merchant Vincent Seve in 1605. Seve was somewhat of a character, professing to live in a hidden cellar within an abandoned quarry so he could better study history and astrology. Seve claimed that a nephew of Nostradamus named Henry called him to come to his death bed, where he bequeathed him a series of Nostradamus's unpublished predictions, which he felt were of the utmost importance. That same year all-new editions of *Les Prophéties* contained these new predictions, dubbed Sixains. Interestingly, these were all markedly different from Nostradamus's other writing, forming six-line verses, with far clearer language and a heavy emphasis on praising France's current king, Henry IV. As you've probably guessed, this is because Seve forged the prophecies, with no historic record of a nephew named Henry existing.

Interest in Nostradamus began to wane towards the end of the seventeenth century. This was, after all, the Age of Enlightenment, of reasoning and science, so there wasn't much place for divination. Yet it birthed the modern use of Nostradamus, appearing at times of great crisis to create both meaning and fear, whether real or not. The first major example of this came during the French Revolution when a particular prophecy was popularized through both press and pamphlets: '*Before too long all things shall be ordained, we sense a sinister age on its way, the state of marks and seals shall be most changed, few to be content with their stations.*' Thanks to its unclear language, it was initially seized upon by both sides of the revolutionary divide. It could mean '*the revolution will be hard but the revolutionaries will win*' or '*the revolutionaries may succeed at first but it would not last for long*'. New editions of *Les Prophéties* were keen to cash in, creating new prophecies that nuns and priests would become targets of the revolution, with these forged verses being internationally reported as fact in 1790. Soon came the individual lies. In 1792, the French press reported that a man had broken into Nostradamus's tomb and found even more prophecies for the year ahead – although he was long dead, it appeared the seer's skeleton was still able to see the future. This was elaborated on in 1794, when it was claimed that National Guard volunteers had also broken into the tomb and found a handwritten note by Nostradamus predicting the emancipation of France.

In more modern history, there was another peak of interest in the run-up to the Second World War, with numerous reprints and 'new' Nostradamus prophecies being printed internationally. During the war itself, sales of *Les Prophéties* boomed and Joseph Goebbels started to use fabricated Nostradamus prophecies as a form of Nazi propaganda against Allied nations. And this has become Nostradamus's legacy – his name used as both crutch and weapon during times of mass crisis. No matter the truth of his original work, today it is mired in centuries' worth of fabrications, making it ever harder to tell what Michel de Nostredame truly claimed to see.

The Imjin War and the Worst Peace Negotiations in History

· ·

Born the son of a Japanese peasant farmer in 1536, Toyotomi Hideyoshi had done whatever he'd needed to defy his means, rising from the ranks of foot soldier to become a samurai and military leader. Throughout the mid-1580s, he'd led a campaign to unify Japan after more than a century of political fragmentation, and now in 1591 he was the country's de facto leader, earning the moniker 'Great Unifier'. Yet Hideyoshi still wanted more, and perhaps his greatest dream was to conquer Ming China – taking down Asia's powerhouse and proving the strength of this new Japan. The best way to attack would be to send forces through Joseon Korea and across China's border.

Hideyoshi had emissaries ask for Korea's permission to pass through. However, Korea was never going to accept; after all, it was a tributary state to Ming China. Still, Seonjo, the fourteenth King of the Joseon dynasty, had his own delegates try to investigate Hideyoshi's plans, but their information wasn't exactly solid. Some reports said that Hideyoshi had a large army that would attack if they weren't allowed to pass through, while others stated that Japan was all talk and would never attack Korea. Seonjo decided to go with the latter and carried on as normal – this would be a big mistake. In April 1592, Japanese troops landed at Busan and laid siege to the city. Within just a few weeks, Hideyoshi had captured the capital,

Hanseong (now known as Seoul). As the invasion worsened, China readied itself to intervene, and by the middle of 1593, Korean and Chinese forces had successfully pushed back Japan. This began what can best be described as an absolute farce of a peace negotiation.

THE IMMORTAL ADMIRAL

Admiral Yi Sun-sin is often regarded as one of the greatest figures in naval history whose innovations, such as the turtle ship, revolutionized naval warfare in Asia. Between 1592 and 1598, his Korean fleet fought in twenty-three battles against Japan, without suffering a loss.

The obvious obstacle was each country's differing opinions. China and Korea just wanted Hideyoshi's forces out of Korea and away from the Chinese border – negotiating was a much better option than unnecessary bloodshed and costly war. However, the situation for Hideyoshi was more nuanced. At present, he simply couldn't win the war, as Korea had recovered from the shock attack and had pulled out an ace card in the form of one Admiral Yi Sun-sin, whose clever naval tactics were consistently defeating Japan's navy. On top of this, guerrilla militias were closing off Japanese supply lines. Cut out at sea, and short of food and ammunition, Hideyoshi was about to lose – but he didn't see it that way. He just needed time to regroup and peace negotiations offered that. In his mind, either the negotiations would end in China and Korea apologizing to Japan and recognizing his might, or he'd just restart the war again, his armies refreshed and replenished. And so, in opening negotiations, Hideyoshi prepared a list of seven demands, which included a truce between China and Japan as well as an opening of trade. In addition, Korea would have to swear to never disobey Japan, send a prince and state ministers as hostages, and allow Japanese forces to maintain control over several of its provinces. In a final flourish, Hideyoshi included a letter that pronounced his destiny as a great ruler of '*the four seas*'.

Hideyoshi's demands and letter never made it to China. He'd chosen to trust the negotiations to a group of delegates helmed by Konishi Yukinaga. Yukinaga had helped lead troops during the Imjin War's first invasion and therefore was under no illusions about how dire Japan's situation really was. He knew that if he presented Hideyoshi's demands to China they'd immediately be thrown out and Japan would ultimately be defeated in its invasion. So, he chose to forge a new set of demands under Hideyoshi's name, accompanied by a fake letter in which Hideyoshi prostrated himself at China's mercy. In terms of lying, things weren't going much better on the Chinese and Korean side. Much of their negotiations went through a man called Shen Weijing, who was not only aware of Yukinaga's forgeries but appears to have helped write some. Interestingly, although unaware of this duplicity, the Korean party was very vocal about mistrusting Weijing, believing him to be a *'rogue'* who could easily be compelled to spy for the Japanese. These misgivings weren't helped by Japan attacking the Korean city of Jinju early on in peace negotiations, leading to the deaths of an estimated 60,000 citizens. Still, somehow, the peace negotiations kept on going.

The routine of back-and-forth forgeries and lying continued until by 1595 both parties felt they had their final negotiations in place. Hideyoshi was of the belief that almost all his original demands would be met, and on top of this, he was to be given an investiture that marked him as an equal in the eyes of Ming China. Yes, he would not seize China as he originally planned, but Japan would still be coming out of this strong, recognized as a powerhouse in global affairs. Of course, this wasn't how China saw things. Their letters from Hideyoshi showed a remorseful leader who just wanted peace and the *actual* investiture they had worked up reflected this, including the line *'Now that you have realized with regret how serious was your error'*. Hideyoshi was to remove his forces from Korea, with no land or hostages to be taken, and in return, China would give Hideyoshi the title of King of Japan, *but* he would be barred from tributary trade and expected to obey and respect China in all regards.

In October 1596, Hideyoshi welcomed the Chinese envoys for the investiture ceremony. He wore their gifts of Ming robes and marked the occasion with a feast. The reason for Hideyoshi's cheer was that he had no idea what the Chinese investiture *actually* said – that was until he asked for it to be translated and read aloud. Upon hearing the contents he grew furious and threatened to kill his negotiators. He'd been made a fool of and, in retaliation, he started the war up once more. By August 1597, Japanese soldiers and ships were headed once again to Busan. But this time, Korea wasn't taken by surprise and their forces proved fierce. Yet, despite the ferociousness of each side, the Imjin War would end unspectacularly. In September 1598, Hideyoshi died, and with his death there really was not much point in continuing the war. Japan ordered its soldiers to return and that was that. Each country was left in debt, with hundreds of thousands of people dead – a fate that may have been avoided if not for perhaps well-intentioned, but poorly executed deceit.

THE THREE DMITRYS

. . . .

While the Imjin War was stopping and starting, Russia was grappling with its own host of problems that had spawned following the death of Ivan the Terrible in 1584. One of the most controversial rulers in Russian history, Ivan was born into a Russia that in 1530 was nowhere near the country we know today. Then called the Grand Principality of Moscow, or Muscovy, it was founded in 1263 as a vassal state under the Mongol Empire and was relatively tiny. This began to change under the rules of Ivan's grandfather and father – Ivan III (1462–1505) and Vasili III (1505–33). In 1480, Ivan III proved victorious over the Great Horde, effectively eradicating any remaining Mongol power and reclaiming independence.

This kicked off something called *'gathering the lands of Rus'*, essentially annexing nearby lands to build up what would become Russia. Ivan III dreamed that Muscovy would become *'The Third Rome'*, a large empire under one ruler – this was the inheritance given to Ivan the Terrible when in 1547, at the age of just sixteen, he was crowned the first Tsar of Russia.

Ivan's reign was a mixed bag to say the least. The beginning of his rule could be called a success: Ivan consolidated autocratic rule, expanded Russia's territory, and adopted more rigorous religious authority. This came at a great cost – sacrificing individual freedom and rights to the interest of the state. However, at least for Ivan and the consolidation of Russia's power, it was a win. Yet this all started to fall apart in 1558 when Ivan set his sights on gaining control over the Baltic Sea and commenced the Livonian War. This would wind up raging for the next twenty-five years, pitting Ivan against Poland–Lithuania, Denmark–Norway and Sweden. As if this wasn't tough enough, in 1560, Ivan's wife, Anastasia Romanovna, died in an apparent assassination. Ivan blamed the Russian aristocracy (known as boyars) for her death, and in a paranoid fit of rage, he planned a particularly bloody and elaborate form of revenge. Russia was cleaved in two, Ivan setting up a separate state known as the Oprichnina in 1565. This region largely consisted of the nation's richest areas, where many boyars lived. To maintain a brutal form of rule, Ivan installed a type of secret police known as the Oprichniki, who had free rein to murder, torture and desecrate as they pleased. Unsurprisingly, this all may have been great for Ivan's revenge scheme but it wasn't good for Russia. Already stretched thin thanks to the Livonian War, now even more resources were being funnelled into maintaining the Oprichnina, leaving the country vulnerable. In 1571, this weakness was fully taken advantage of, when Crimean Tartars successfully stormed Moscow, burning down great swathes of the city, enslaving many of its people and killing thousands of others.

Ivan's revenge had left Russia on its knees and to survive the country had to unite once more. The Oprichnina operation was shut down and efforts once again returned to war – but it was too little, too late. The Livonian War ended in 1583, and Russia was essentially forced into peace negotiations that left them with no net gains from their twenty-five years of fighting. When Ivan died a year later, Russia was barely hanging on. Sure, he'd expanded its borders early on and much of that land remained – but its people, its economy and its morale were in tatters. Russia needed a strong heir to lead them to salvation. The problem was, that heir was dead. Ivan the Terrible's eldest son, Ivan Ivanovich, had been bred to take on the mantle of Russia; however, in 1581, Ivan had killed him in a fit of rage. This left only two sons remaining – Feodor, who likely had an intellectual disability as well as no interest in governance, and Dmitry, who was an infant. What would become known as the Time of Troubles was about to begin.

Feodor became tsar, but unable to lead, his brother-in-law and former counsel for Ivan the Terrible, Boris Godunov, was named de facto regent. Boris's rule was actually fairly effective, but his grip on power was very rocky and by 1591 Feodor still had no children, meaning that young Dmitry was the only true successor to the throne. It didn't take a genius to work out that this made the now eight-year-old boy a threat. Which is perhaps why, when in May 1591, Dmitry was found dead with his throat slit, the first thought was an assassination. However, the official cause given was that Dmitry had either slit his own throat or fallen onto an upended knife during an epileptic fit – but nobody really believed that. Still, the last heir was dead and this left the door open for Boris – when Feodor died in 1598, Tsar Boris ascended the throne.

A GODUNOV LEADER

Despite having almost certainly signed off on killing a child, as a ruler Boris Godunov wasn't actually that bad, blighted more by bad luck and a tenuous tie to power than ineffectual ruling. In fact, he was arguably the first tsar to form strong contact with the rest of Europe, declaring, '*All nations are equally appealing to him, that he wants to live in friendship with everyone*' – unless, of course, your name was Dmitry.

Boris proved unpopular. In 1601, Russia had been gripped by a famine that over the course of three years would kill around 2 million people, and the blame for this was placed squarely at Boris's door. As if things couldn't get any worse for the new tsar, in 1604, something very strange happened – Dmitry returned.

Well, at least someone who said they were Dmitry. Now known as False Dmitry I, the young man claimed to have escaped the assassination attempt by fleeing and leaving behind a lookalike who'd been killed in his place. Now he was back and he wanted his throne. This wasn't just a throwaway threat, as False Dmitry I had real power behind him in the shape of the Polish–Lithuanian Commonwealth. Poland–Lithuania knew that this was an imposter, but they were keen to overthrow Boris and take a slice of Russian power. In March 1605, False Dmitry I marched upon Russia, preparing himself to battle for the crown – this wouldn't be necessary. In late April, Boris died, likely from a stroke, leaving his teenage son Feodor II as the new tsar. Feodor was almost immediately murdered and by June, Tsar Dmitry was on the throne.

The false Dmitry's reign actually started very well. He had the support of the people and the boyars, who despite initially claiming him an imposter, now vouched for his credibility. Dmitry set out plans to improve life for Russia's peasants and continue the tradition of gathering the lands of Rus by putting in place alliances and seeking war with the Ottoman Empire. Yet this would be incredibly short-lived. On 8 May 1606, Dmitry married Marina Mniszech, who was Catholic, and made it clear she didn't plan on converting to Orthodox Christianity. This angered the powerful Russian Church and caused the boyars to turn on Dmitry – declaring him (yet again) an imposter. Less than ten days later, on 17 May, Dmitry was murdered, and by 19 May, the head of the boyars, Vasili Shuisky, was the new tsar.

The parade of Dmitrys did not end though. In 1607, another one popped up (False Dmitry II). He had somehow survived his murder, and despite not looking anything like the first false Dmitry, was officially recognized by Marina Mniszech as her husband. Once more Poland–Lithuania offered their support and by 1608 Dmitry II had forces tens of thousands strong, which included peasantry as well as several boyars who had defected from Vasili. Unfortunately for the imposter, he wouldn't get to become tsar. Poland decided that there was enough unrest now that it could just directly declare war, and in 1609, King Sigismund III did just that. Dmitry's Polish forces were directed elsewhere, and though he desperately tried to cling to that tsardom dream, he was killed during a drunken fight in 1610.

The war raged on, and by 1610, Polish forces were in Moscow and Tsar Vasili was deposed. Another Dmitry (False Dmitry III) appeared in 1611, but this time, nobody really believed in the myth of what would have been his third miraculous survival and although he gained a little rebel support, he was swiftly betrayed and executed. It wouldn't be until 1612 and the Battle of Moscow that Russia once again regained its foothold and a new tsar was elected Michael Romanov. This would mark the end of the Time of Troubles and the beginning of the Romanov rule of Russia. Yet the Dmitry saga itself was still not at an end. Marina Mniszech had escaped the fate of False Dmitry II and now claimed that her four-year-old son, Ivan Dmitriyevich, was the true Tsar of Russia. It was a bizarre move and one that had very little support, yet Michael knew by now that false Dmitrys could be a deadly threat. Marina and her son were captured, and she would die in prison, but Michael ordered Ivan to be publicly executed, bringing a swift and bloody end to this imposter lineage.

THE AFFAIR OF THE POISONS

In the late 1670s, a very strange hysteria rocked France, with rumours of secret underground poisoning rings, demonic black masses, and even love potions being used to buy power. As fear spread, a witch hunt was sparked within the highest echelons possible – the court of Louis XIV. What makes this frenzy even more peculiar is that, unlike other witch hunts, it wasn't based on religion or a social crisis but was rooted in what may seem like a very modern obsession – true crime. In 1673, it was discovered that for almost a decade the dainty aristocrat, the Marquise de Brinvilliers, had been systematically killing off her family, stealthily dosing her father and two brothers with poison over weeks and months until each died from what was at first considered to be a long, albeit mysterious illness. The motive for their murders was primarily greed, the Marquise hoping to cash in on her inheritance as well as being able to continue seeing her lover, who her father and brothers disapproved of. Indeed, it wasn't until her lover died in 1672 that evidence of the crimes was first found after debtors looted his home. The Marquise fled but was eventually caught, tried and executed in 1676.

The story of the Marquise murders was a much-celebrated scandal, but it went beyond a macabre piece of gossip. If the Marquise de Brinvilliers could pull off such a heinous crime, then so could anyone – full-blown hysteria broke out. As fear took hold, some saw an opportunity to get rich quick. Of this number was Magdelaine de La Grange, who operated as one of Paris's leading fortune tellers, specializing in using divination to tell clients if they had been poisoned (for which she provided a pricey antidote). In 1677, she was arrested for trying to forge a marriage claim to the elderly lawyer Jean Fauyre, in order to gain an inheritance, with the man dying not long after. Poisoning was suspected. In a bid to get out of prison, Magdelaine professed to having knowledge of potential crimes of national importance, and the French Minister of War, the Marquis de Louvois, was drafted in to check out her claims. Magdelaine reported that Fauyre had indeed been poisoned, but not by her – a secret plot to assassinate the king and dauphin was underway and Fauyre had been just one of its victims. Although Magdelaine had no further information, she swore that if freed from prison her clairvoyant powers would be able to find out more. Louvois didn't bite, but then new evidence came to light when in late 1677 an alchemist and his manservant were arrested for forgery. The servant told jailers that in return for a pardon he would offer information about a plot concerning the king. With this and Magdelaine's bid for freedom in mind, Louvois believed he'd come across something extraordinary – a Parisian poisoning ring.

With King Louis XIV appearing to be at the heart of this supposed plot, it was imperative to capture its participants, but beyond Magdelaine and the alchemist's associates, Louvois had hit a wall. That was until January 1679, when two fortune tellers, Marie Bosse and Marie Vigoreux, were arrested after allegedly being overheard joking about their poisoning successes. A search of Bosse's home found arsenic and other poisons, not exactly uncommon for household cleaning and pest management, but enough to spark fear when combined with the fact that Madame de Poulaillon, an upper-class client of both women, had recently been moved to a convent after it was suspected she'd tried to poison her husband. Louvois appeared to have finally found the ring, and an investigation began in the belief that Parisian fortune tellers were working with aristocratic women to bump off their husbands and rivals.

By March, the caseloads had piled up so much that Louis XIV ordered the creation of a special commission to handle it all. Meanwhile, the newly incarcerated fortune tellers were realizing just how precarious their position was, with Magdelaine de La Grange having been executed in February 1679. Desperate to prove their innocence, the prisoners began pointing the finger at anyone else, that blame often being laid at the feet of the most notorious and well known of them all, Catherine Montvoisin (known as La Voisin), whose clients included France's most elite aristocrats. Allegations of poisonings advanced well beyond simple drink spiking to poisoned bouquets and clothing, soon tumbling into the wilds of witchcraft, black masses and demonic powers. The prisoners were willing to say anything to earn their freedom, but for many this blame game would prove fruitless, only leading their interrogations to progress to torture in hopes

THE MYSTERIOUS DEATH OF
HENRIETTA OF ENGLAND

Part of the reason for the court of Louis XIV becoming so obsessed with the poisoning scandal was the death of the king's sister-in-law Henrietta Anne, who'd died in 1670 after a short but sudden illness. There had been rumours at the time but now people were sure that she had to have been poisoned; after all, if nowhere was safe, then the halls of power and ambition had to be the deadliest place of all.

they'd spill more secrets – which in turn led to more false confessions and allegations.

This environment of fear is perhaps what led La Voisin to finally make her own accusations, naming clients she said had demanded poison from her, the most scandalous linked name being that of Françoise de Dreux, whose whole family crammed the king's court. La Voisin was by far the most connected suspect and, as such, it was hoped that she held the key to whatever danger the king was in. And so, when in May 1679, Bosse, Vigoreux, and several others were executed or died under torture, La Voisin was spared. Between La Voisin and the newer suspects, a number of the royal court's most notable staples were accused of everything from murder to summoning the devil. However, it soon became clear that La Voisin had run out of names to give, and her information was rapidly reducing to seemingly mundane titbits, such as once hoping to personally hand a petition to the king. Finding no further use for her, in February 1680, La Voisin was summarily executed. Still, her death didn't immediately appear to change the hysteria thriving at the royal court – the only way to quell it would be to name the person who Magdelaine de La Grange had once alleged threatened the king.

Interrogators set their sights on a curious party – the king's mistress, the Marquise de Montespan. She'd been on the radar for a little while, with several of her associates named in the investigation; however, to charge the king's paramour and mother of his children would be a risky business, requiring far more weight behind it – they needed new allegations and the interrogators would get these by whatever means necessary. For this an unusual witness was found – La Voisin's daughter.

Marguerite Montvoisin had been arrested shortly before her mother's death, on the simple basis that she was related to La Voisin. She had not fared well in prison, attempting suicide at least once, and by the summer of 1680, she was known to be mentally unstable and highly suggestible. When called in for questioning, Marguerite happily parroted back what interrogators asked or made up lies to fill in their gaps. This first benefitted the investigation when Marguerite claimed that the petition her mother had mentioned had actually been poisoned, part of an elaborate plot to kill the king. After this bombshell, she was interrogated again and again. Although her testimony often vastly varied and contradicted itself, interrogators used it to paint their own picture – de Montespan had used La Voisin for years to dose the king with love potions, spells and black masses to strengthen his adoration. However, when the king's eye wandered to the Duchess of Fontanges, she plotted both their murders, with La Voisin to deliver the poisoned petition and a poisoned cloth to be used to dispatch Fontanges not long after.

When the investigation was presented to Louis XIV, he remained unsure. Despite everything laid before him, he still had feelings for de Montespan and so requested further digging. The problem was that the more interrogations and torture happened, the wilder the prisoners' accusations became, with human sacrifice soon becoming part of the case. On top of this, by the end of 1680, the frenzy that had once gripped the royal court had blown over. Nobody beyond the king and interrogators knew about the allegations against de Montespan and it had been months since the last wave of arrests – in the court's mind everything had long since been resolved. If Louis XIV were to charge de Montespan, he'd be beginning the cycle again in addition to saying that demonic witchcraft, sacrifice and murder had been de rigueur at his court, claims which his advisers pointed out had little evidence or grounding, beyond mostly forced and desperate confessions. The hysteria was over – why open it up again?

Louis XIV decided to hold off on making a decision. That was until the Duchess of Fontanges left the French court in March 1681. For months she'd been suffering from a mysterious illness and was told she would die soon. Of course, rumours of poisoning soon sprang up. Perhaps with this in mind, Louis finally determined that the commission's investigation would go forward, but with all mention of the Marquise de Montespan omitted. For those still imprisoned, trials began in July, and prisoners were divided into those who could be charged without mention of de Montespan and those who could not. Of the former, most were executed or exiled, allowing a bloody show to prove that the last perpetrators had been caught. Meanwhile, the latter, including Marguerite Montvoisin were imprisoned for life to ensure the whole affair remained behind closed doors. In 1682, Louis ordered the commission to be shut down and with that, the once all-consuming fatal flurry of lies was consigned to the footnotes of history.

MARY TOFT: THE WOMAN WHO BIRTHED RABBITS

On 10 October 1726, British newspapers began to report on a most extraordinary story – a young woman named Mary Toft had just given birth to a rabbit. This was of course not true. The whole thing was a very curious hoax and it wasn't even put together well enough to stand up to more than a few weeks of scrutiny – by December, the whole scam had been rumbled. Now this might sound like a fanciful if easily forgotten farce, but Mary and her rabbits were significant, so much so that they would move the understanding of medicine forward.

Born in 1703, Mary married Joshua Toft when she was seventeen. The couple lived in the small town of Godalming and often found themselves on the poverty line. Joshua's work as a wool-cloth-trader was hit by a depression in the industry and the couple scraped by on his meagre earnings and Mary's work as an agricultural day labourer. Now, we don't know exactly why Mary went from day labourer to rabbit birther. At the time, and in the centuries after, it was assumed she did it to make a quick buck, despite Mary having never actually profited from the hoax. In recent years, the historian Karen Harvey has re-examined the case and believes that the hoax had less to do with Mary seeking ill-gotten gains and more to do with her reaction to the environment she was living in.

Rabbits were actually a prominent feature in Mary's life well before the hoax began. Godalming was overseen by multiple levels of governance that had control over the day-to-day lives of the poor in particular, including overseeing rent, punishment and even policing the reproduction rates of women like Mary. Animals such as rabbits, deer and fish were a frequently used symbol of this landowning elite, who on top of everything else, restricted the poor from being able to access this plentiful food source. There was an added issue to this – rabbits, in particular, would often roam into the fields that the poor's livelihood depended on, eating crops and livestock's food. Protests around this kind of activity were common and, in the summer of 1726, Joshua was actually in one, joining a mass trespass to fish in a prohibited pond, which was treated as a crime. At the same time as this, Mary tragically suffered a miscarriage. She'd given birth twice before, with only one of her children surviving beyond infancy – something that was noted by Godalming's elite. This miscarriage lasted for several weeks, with Mary having no choice but to work in the fields throughout. She later recalled that at one point, she spotted a rabbit running through the field and chased after it, desperate to catch it for food. After this, she claimed, she could not stop thinking about rabbits. In the weeks after her miscarriage, Mary still appeared to be pregnant, and several historians now believe that the community took advantage of this, having Mary appear to give birth to rabbits as another protest aimed at the landowning elite, not only for the restrictions on poaching but also their control over women.

No matter the true intended reason behind the hoax, by October, news was spreading across the country of the woman that birthed rabbits. In November, King George I sent his court anatomist, Nathaniel St André, to investigate the phenomenon. As luck would have it, when St André visited Mary, she was in the midst of 'birthing' her fifteenth rabbit. The anatomist took in the incredible sight and immediately ordered that Mary be transported to London so her miraculous births could be studied by the greatest scientific minds of the day. It was thought that Mary may well be the perfect embodiment of the idea of 'Maternal Impression', a popular emerging theory within medicine at the time. Maternal Impression was the idea that what a mother experienced during pregnancy would impact the child she gave birth to. In 1724, Scottish physician John Maubray detailed the theory in his book, *The Female Physician*. He argued that a woman's imagination was a powerful thing, so if a mother had pregnancy cravings for mussels, then her baby might look like a shellfish, while depression or trauma could result in deformities, and even a cherry falling on a woman during pregnancy could result in birth marks. Mary Toft had thought of nothing but rabbits and, thus, she had birthed rabbits.

Maubray examined Mary and thought himself vindicated; Nathaniel St André was also quick to cash in, publishing a paper on Mary's births within a month of meeting her. But their success wouldn't last for long. A porter at the London house where Mary was staying reported that she was smuggling rabbits into her rooms. Mary denied the claims but was told the only way to set the record straight was to undergo surgery – she burst into tears and admitted the whole thing had been a hoax. The British press had a field day, dragging Mary and the physicians who'd believed her through the mud. As punishment Mary was publicly detained and for a small fee crowds could pay to have her paraded in front of them as they jeered. After her release, Mary returned home, where she

---

MISJUDGED MATERNITY

One of the most known people whose birth was supposedly intertwined with Maternal Impression was Joseph Merrick, or as he is also known, the Elephant Man, who was born in 1862. His mother claimed to have been startled by an elephant while pregnant, which resulted in his physical deformities. Modern science has debunked this, but Merrick's condition remains unknown, though some hypothesize it to have been a combination of Proteus syndrome and Neurofibromatosis.

---

gave birth to a healthy baby girl and quietly lived out the rest of her life.

The medical community continued to suffer, causing mass distrust and becoming a public mockery for their willingness to believe the unbelievable. Ironically though, the idea of Maternal Impression continued. A few doctors published papers using the Mary Toft saga to disprove the theory, but, if anything, it strangely appeared to have made it more fascinating. In the years immediately afterwards, several reports were filed with strikingly similar cases, including a woman whose pregnancy craving for cake resulted in a child that looked like the baked good (currants and all), as well as another woman whose child was part frog. As late as the 1890s, the *British Medical Journal* was still reporting on these kinds of 'monstrous' births. Mary Toft's hoax may have been immediately called out as a fake but it would take decades for the weird science she inadvertently pushed to receive the same judgement.

THE LIE OF MIR JAFAR

There is a popular story that India became colonized by the British thanks to one man and his lies. In 1757, at the Battle of Plassey, Mir Jafar Ali Khan, a once-respected general, double-crossed his leader and his people, handing control of Bengal to England's East India Company and setting forth centuries of oppressive colonization. But this isn't entirely true; after all, history is nothing if not incredibly complicated. In fact, the tale of Mir Jafar is in itself a lie, hiding the true nature of this double cross and the players behind it. But to get to that truth we first have to look at how the East India Company went from bungling its way into relations with India to vying to become a global superpower.

On 31 December 1600, Queen Elizabeth I granted a royal charter to the newly formed East India Company. Trade in exotic goods such as spices, silks and jewels was big business, and this charter entitled the company to a monopoly over the English trade as well as the right to seize land and form armies in name of queen and country. The latter rights initially wouldn't seem to be useful for the East India Company's hopes of trading with India.

At this point in time, much of the Indian subcontinent, home to one of the world's most lucrative markets, was ruled by the rich and powerful Mughal dynasty. No other European traders had been able to truly crack India, as the Mughals wouldn't tolerate their usual practices of plundering land and forcing conversions to Christianity on locals. With forces roughly 4 million strong, they could crush badly behaved traders with very little bother. So the East India Company began a lengthy campaign of buttering up the Mughal emperor, Jahangir. Surrounded by lavish jewels and wealth, the company couldn't shower Jahangir with impressive gifts that he didn't already have and instead opted to send royal envoys and regaled him with tales of English curiosities such as beer and fog. Amused by their antics, Jahangir granted the company trading rights and soon their fortunes were flourishing, expanding across the Mughal Empire.

However, although on the surface relations looked good, the East India Company was secretly simmering at not being deferred to. By the 1680s, the Mughal Empire was under attack from the Maratha Confederacy, and sensing that their master was weakening, the East India Company tried to seize control. In an incredibly poorly thought-out bout of pride, in 1686, nineteen warships and six hundred soldiers were sent to take on the Mughal dynasty – they were immediately quashed and the company's trade was shut down. This should have just been a blip on the historic radar; after all, it only took four years of desperate apologizing for the Mughals to forgive the young upstart traders. However, following the trade shutdown, whilst rebuilding their infrastructure, the East

India Company made a land acquisition that would prove something of a game changer – a then mostly empty swathe of land in Bengal called Calcutta (now known as Kolkata).

By the start of the 1700s, it was clear that the once-mighty Mughal Empire was falling apart. The reign of Emperor Aurangzeb had massively weakened the country. His penalization of Hindus and escalation of Sharia law caused a great religious gulf within his people, which combined with multiple military failures left the empire weak and open to attack. Following Aurangzeb's death in 1707, the country fell into fractured sections, disparate and frequently unorganized. This was all great news for the East India Company who now had carte blanche to do whatever they wanted. Wars were fought with France and their traders to capture each other's lands, with the East India Company frequently coming out on top. Meanwhile, Calcutta had become a thriving business hub with almost two-thirds of the company's Asian exports coming through the port city by the 1750s. This was in stark contrast to much of the rest of Bengal, which had spent 1741–51 struggling under invasions from the Marathas. As refugees poured into Calcutta, the East India Company continued doing its own thing, refusing to pay taxes and contemplating bringing Bengal to war with France and its traders. This did not go down well with Bengal's ruler, the Nawab of Bengal, Alivardi Khan. In a bid to avoid bloodshed, Alivardi sent envoys to try to come to a diplomatic understanding – the company laughed out these attempts. In April 1756, Alivardi died and his successor, Siraj ud-Daulah, decided enough was enough. In late May, he led thousands of men to lay siege to the company's factory in Kadimbazaar. When the East India Company still didn't back down, Siraj and his now 70,000-strong force marched on Calcutta.

At the head of this campaign was Mir Jafar, who commanded the troops as they arrived at the city gates on 16 June. Within a day they were making their way through Calcutta, and by the 19th, the East India Company had lost control, the governor fleeing and leaving his remaining men to their fates. The loss of Calcutta was a huge blow to the company; their stock had been plundered; hundreds had died; and, more importantly, their share price was tumbling. After many a furious board meeting, it was decided that the company had to strike back, not only reclaiming Calcutta but taking Bengal itself as compensation for lost business. Led by company man Robert Clive, a monumental force was formed, far outstripping Siraj and his own tens of thousands. On 2 January 1757, they won back Calcutta, but with huge losses on both sides. Still, Robert Clive had been tasked with taking Bengal and so, ever the loyal worker, he declared war on Siraj ud-Daulah. Despite the company's weakened forces, Siraj was surprisingly quick to back down, fleeing during a night raid. By February, a peace treaty was signed that essentially entitled the company to go back to doing whatever they pleased. But with the ink on the treaty barely dry, a curve ball was thrown – France and England had declared war on each other. Any land gained was a win and so Clive was commanded to take his tired troops to snatch French trading lands.

THE BLACK HOLE

One of the most notorious aspects of Siraj ud-Daulah's march on Calcutta was the infamous Black Hole of Calcutta, where on 20 June 1756, approximately 146 of the British left behind were forced into a cell measuring 18 feet by 14 feet, 10 inches. Over the course of the night, many of the prisoners suffocated, were crushed, or died of heat exhaustion, with an alleged 123 of the 146 dead by morning.

Meanwhile, those around Siraj ud-Daulah were close to calling a coup. Mir Jafar and his military men were disgusted at how quickly Siraj had thrown in the towel, while Bengal's banking dynasty, the Jaget Seths, were furious at Siraj bleeding Bengal dry. Both parties waited for Siraj to announce he was breaking the treaty and offering support to the French, eradicating the East India Company once and for all. But he didn't and England proved victorious, expanding their Bengal territory even further. Siraj had to go. Yet every scheme to oust Siraj failed until, finally, the plotters became desperate – perhaps, the enemy of their enemy might just be their friend. Hearing of the plotters' plan, the East India Company held a secret meeting in May 1757 and agreed to help remove Siraj from power – but they wouldn't do it for free. In return for their forces, they demanded Bengal pay up an entire year's worth of its income. The plotters agreed.

The plan was this: Robert Clive would accuse Siraj of breaking their treaty, giving the company forces an excuse to strike. Following Siraj's death, Mir Jafar would become leader, the face of a military man, far better than that of a banker. All Mir Jafar had to do now was ensure that, when the company's troops arrived, Siraj was front and centre for the taking. Except, Mir Jafar didn't. In mid-June, as Clive marched towards Plassey, where Siraj was entrenched, he kept writing to Mir Jafar for an update on his end, but he got no response. On 18 June, Mir Jafar was meant to join the company troops but never showed. Clive kept on pursuing the general, only getting the response that he'd opted to stay by Siraj's side to avoid suspicion before silence resumed once more. By 21 June, a frustrated Clive was holding a war council on whether the plan was even going ahead, upon which Mir Jafar delivered a message to say that he was still ready to strike, before promptly disappearing again. On 23 June, with no sign of Mir Jafar, Clive decided to finally end the farce and fight – the Battle of Plassey commenced. As cannons fired, the general ultimately appeared for long enough to withdraw his troops and help seal a victory for the company. Siraj fled, but was caught a few days later and killed.

The double cross had worked, despite Mir Jafar seeming to have last-minute reservations. By July he had been declared the new Nawab of Bengal, and the bankers began the process of paying back the East India Company. However, it didn't take long for the double-crossers to be double-crossed. The company had essentially bought itself a revolution and as such had a stranglehold over those who'd taken part. They'd transformed from traders to the true power behind a puppet ruler. Unsurprisingly, the people of Bengal didn't love Mir Jafar; he'd killed his leader, teamed up with the enemy to do so, and decimated the economy in the process, not to mention that the former general was now addicted to opium. Still, Mir Jafar's failed leadership was another win for the company, allowing them to further extort Bengal. Far from saving Bengal, the plotters' scheme had if anything further ruined it, and by 1759 both Mir Jafar and the Jaget Seths were desperately seeking a way to get rid of the East India Company.

The first port of call was the Dutch East India Company, who were promised trading rights to Bengal if they could get rid of the company; however, they were defeated at the Battle of Chinsurah, triggering the overthrow of Mir Jafar and his replacement by a new puppet ruler, Mir Qasim. But there was another hope, a Mughal emperor remained, Shah Alam II, and although his empire had all but crumbled, he still had support.

In 1759, some of the last French troops in north India pledged to join Shah Alam in taking down the East India Company. Mir Qasim had also turned against the company, thanks to them, yet again, refusing to pay taxes. Battles, skirmishes and sieges broke out and in an ironic twist, the company replaced Mir Qasim with the now far more docile drug-addled Mir Jafar. It all culminated in 1764's Battle of Buxar. The fight was short but bloody, the East India Company victorious. This win was arguably the greatest turning point in establishing British rule over India. The last vestiges of Mughal rule had been defeated and the company was given administration and taxation rights over Bengal making them the de facto rulers. In 1765, Mir Jafar died and in telling the company directors the news, Robert Clive wrote: '*It is scarce hyperbole to say that whole empire is in our hands.*' It now truly was.

Joseph Knight's Fight for Freedom

By the late 1700s, one of the British Empire's flagships of trade was Jamaica. English forces first conquered the Caribbean island in 1655 and by 1707 it had been declared a British colony. A hub for sugarcane plantations, the success of its colonial masters relied on the slave trade, and between 1655 and the end of the slave trade in 1809, an estimated 600,000 people were transported from Africa to Jamaica and forced into slavery. One of these slaves was a thirteen-year-old boy, who in early 1765 had been kidnapped from his home, torn from his family, and imprisoned with 290 others aboard the slaver ship, the *Phoenix*. In April, the *Phoenix* landed in Montego Bay, Jamaica, and began selling off its human cargo. The ship's captain, John Knight, took the boy and privately sold him to the Scottish plantation owner Sir John Wedderburn, who gave the young teen a new name – Joseph Knight (the surname a nod to his kidnapper, Captain Knight).

Wedderburn wasn't only in Jamaica to earn his fortune, he was also on the run. His father, the 5th Baronet of Blackness, had been executed for treason following a Jacobite uprising, and not wanting to meet the same fate, Wedderburn had fled Scotland in 1747. Since then, he'd become one of the largest plantation owners in Jamaica, his sugar operation earning him riches beyond belief. Wedderburn hoped that this new fortune would help him not only return to Scotland but reclaim his family's place in the nobility. Joseph Knight was to be a pawn in this plan – black servants were seen as a sign of wealth in Britain, and so Wedderburn would *'breed'* Joseph to become his manservant. Joseph was trained up, taught how to read and write in both French and English, and within three years was back on another ship, this time to set sail for Scotland.

Wet and windy, Scotland was like nothing Joseph had ever experienced before, and although Wedderburn's plans for a return to status had worked for him, not much changed for Joseph, bar his new environment. Working in Wedderburn's Ballindean Estate in Perthshire, Joseph remained a manservant but was separate from the household's other servants – still a slave and bound to Wedderburn. But this was all about to change, thanks to a landmark legal case in England. In November 1771, a slave named James Somerset was bound in chains to be transported from London to Jamaica, where he'd be resold. Somerset had only recently arrived in England, having spent much of his life enslaved in America, but travelled to London in 1769 with his master, Charles Steuart. Not long after landing in the city, Somerset escaped, but now recaptured, his punishment was to be once more sold into slavery. Fortunately, an abolitionist group got involved and reported that Somerset had been illegally imprisoned. In 1772, an English court found that there was no legal precedent for Somerset's detention and so he was released. This was big news, reported far and wide, with some newspaper headlines declaring that the Somerset case would likely put an end to slavery within Britain and give slaves who, like Somerset, had been bought in other countries and later taken to Britain, the right to leave their masters. Sadly, what the press was saying wasn't actually true. The judge's ruling for James Somerset had been deliberately vague; it didn't state any meaningful change to slavery as a system, or even suggest that James Somerset was no longer a slave, just that Charles Steuart couldn't detain or resell him. Still – that wasn't what the papers were saying.

In July 1772, Joseph Knight read about the Somerset case in a local newspaper and believed that this meant that, legally, he should be freed. Interestingly, this wasn't the first time Joseph had looked into the possibility of freedom. In 1768, after landing in Scotland, Joseph had asked Wedderburn if he might now be paid or offered freedom. Wedderburn promised Joseph that in seven years he'd be freed. A year later, Wedderburn further added to this, vowing that on freeing Joseph, he would grant him land and a home in Jamaica. But as 1772 turned to 1773, Joseph was beginning to doubt Wedderburn's word. He'd been patiently waiting for his master to acknowledge the Somerset case and grant his freedom; but it never happened and although at first Joseph hadn't wanted to rock the boat, now he had another reason to fight.

Joseph had fallen in love with one of Wedderburn's servants, Ann Thompson. Ann was likely white and so the couple initially kept their relationship secret; however, Ann soon became pregnant. The pair secretly married but their bliss was short-lived. On discovering Ann's pregnancy, Wedderburn fired her, and desperate to care for his young family, Joseph appealed to Wedderburn to finally grant him his freedom. Joseph didn't actually want to stop working for Wedderburn, he just wanted to get paid – Wedderburn refused. Finally, Joseph realized that Wedderburn had been lying to him for years and had never intended to set him free. And so, Joseph freed himself. In his mind, he'd been legally free since 1772, he'd just been playing it safe by waiting for Wedderburn to declare it. In November 1773, Joseph Knight resigned, took his family, and left the Ballindean Estate. Almost immediately, a warrant for his arrest was issued.

On 15 November, Joseph was apprehended and the courts found in Wedderburn's favour – the escaped slave must return to his master. But Joseph didn't. During proceedings Wedderburn had admitted he'd never planned to free Joseph, enslaving him until either Joseph or he died. To Joseph, this was a smoking gun – proving Wedderburn's lies and that he was ignoring the precedent set by the Somerset case. So Joseph saved up every scrap of money he could get and in 1774 he did the unthinkable – he took his master to court.

AVOIDING ABOLITION

The Slave Trade Abolition Act of March 1807 would abolish Britain's participation in the transatlantic slave trade; however, it wouldn't be until 1833 that the Slavery Abolition Act was passed. That's not to say such abuse of human rights ended. Many British colonies in the Caribbean changed to using indentured service from predominantly Chinese and Indian people, with incidences of violence, assault and lack of basic hygiene and care being reported, in addition to high mortality rates.

What makes Joseph's legal fight even more incredible was that much of his argument leaned heavily on his understanding of the Somerset case, which was wholly incorrect. Yet Joseph's adamance and the wide misreporting of James Somerset's ruling meant that it was not only accepted but that the Sheriff of Perth found in favour of Joseph Knight – he was legally a free man. Of course, Wedderburn was not going to let this stand and filed an appeal with Edinburgh's Court of Sessions in 1775. A final ruling wouldn't happen until 1778, but it would prove worth the wait, the judge ruling: '*The state of slavery is not recognised by the laws of this kingdom, and is inconsistent with the principles thereof: That the regulations in Jamaica, concerning slaves, do not extend to this kingdom; and repelled the defender's claim to a perpetual service.*'

Joseph Knight had won. More than that, the wording in his ruling made it clear that it was not legally acceptable to have a slave on Scottish soil, creating a clear safe harbour for any slaves in Scotland who sought freedom. Of course, in practice, things weren't that clean-cut, as some Scottish slave owners completely ignored the ruling, but it was a monumental step forward towards the abolishment of slavery. As for Joseph Knight, we don't know exactly what happened next. He ceased to appear in historic records and, in this case, that's likely a good thing, meaning he didn't find himself in any more trouble. The last we see of Joseph, he was setting off to live a well-deserved quiet life with Ann.

THE LOST DIAMONDS OF MARIE ANTOINETTE

'*Let them eat cake*' are words it's unlikely Marie Antoinette ever said. Still, today this sentence remains her legacy and there's no arguing that she was the poster child of everything the French Revolutionaries stood against. But what pushed Marie

Antoinette into that position wasn't necessarily her lavish lifestyle or expensive taste – it was a scam and a diamond necklace that she didn't even own.

Around 1772, the French king, Louis XV, commissioned Parisian jewellers Boehmer and Bassange to create an elaborate diamond necklace for his mistress Madame du Barry. The piece was to be unparalleled, encrusted with 647 of the finest diamonds money could buy, and cost around £15 million in today's money. Sourcing the jewels and creating the necklace would be a timely pursuit, one that Louis XV never lived to see, having died of smallpox in 1774. Boehmer and Bassange were left with an incredibly expensive necklace and no buyer, so they reached out to the new queen, Marie Antoinette. Yet she refused to purchase the piece, perhaps because it had been intended for her court rival Madame du Barry, though the official reason she gave was that such a great sum would be better spent by her husband, Louis XVI, on naval ships. The jewellers persisted, desperate to get rid of this monetary millstone, but Marie Antoinette would always turn them down. And so the necklace remained in the hands of Boehmer and Bassange, a hefty reminder of the dangers of selling to aged kings. That was until a trickster named Jeanne de Valois set her sights on the diamonds.

Born in 1756, Jeanne de Valois-Saint-Rémy came from nobility, although by now her family were wholly financially ruined, her father having died in a Parisian poor house. This didn't stop her from pursuing glory within the ranks of Frances's highest echelons. She restyled herself as Jeanne de Valois, claiming a link to the French throne through a bastard line. In 1780, she married 'Count' Nicholas de la Motte, a fellow self-proclaimed noble with not a penny to his name. Together the pair schemed to make it to the French court, bringing in a fellow huckster, Nicholas's friend, Jeanne's occasional lover and alleged pimp, Rétaux de Villette.

THE ILL-PLANNED ESCAPADES
OF MADAME DU BARRY

Madame du Barry, the originally intended recipient of the necklace, would actually meet her end partially thanks to her own jewellery heist scandal. After being essentially iced out of the French court by Marie Antoinette, du Barry retired to her lavish chateau, where she quietly lived at the start of the revolution. However, when most of her jewels were stolen in 1791, she began to travel across France and England looking for them, which brought a *lot* of attention. In 1793, she was arrested and beheaded.

In 1783, the couple made the acquaintance of Cardinal de Rohan, the middle-aged former Ambassador to Vienna. Rohan's star had since fallen, having often infuriated Marie Antoinette's mother, Empress Maria Theresa, during his tenure in Vienna and as such wasn't exactly welcome in Marie's court. Still, Rohan was very rich and exceedingly desperate to regain his power – the perfect pawn for Jeanne's plan. She became his mistress and promised Rohan that as Marie Antoinette was her 'cousin' she could patch things up between them. Delighted, Rohan began writing letters begging for the queen's forgiveness, with replies being written and sent back by Rétaux de Villette. However, by 1784, Rohan was starting to get suspicious – he'd been writing to Marie Antoinette for months and yet nothing had changed. To keep him on the hook, the trio found a young sex worker, Nicole Le Guay, who looked a little bit like the queen. Under the cover of night, Nicole was spirited into Versailles gardens to meet with Rohan and assure him of her favour. This actually worked, allowing Jeanne to move in for the kill.

Jeanne informed Rohan that Marie Antoinette was ready to accept him back; however, first, he would need to provide a peace offering of sorts – Boehmer and Bassange's diamond necklace. It was simply too expensive for Marie to buy herself and so Rohan must secretly acquire it for her. The sale went through in February 1785, the cardinal providing Rétaux de Villette's forged letters as proof of the queen's orders. It didn't take long for Jeanne to pocket the necklace, pick it apart and sell off the diamonds on the black market. But the affair didn't stay secret for long, thanks to Boehmer and Bassange cryptically writing to Marie Antoinette to thank her for finally buying the necklace. Understandably, the queen was confused and an investigation was swiftly launched. On 15 August 1785, Cardinal Rohan was arrested at Versailles, and in the following days Jeanne, Nicholas and Rétaux were also rounded up, along with Nicole Le Guay and another conman who'd latched onto the gullible Cardinal, magician and supposed psychic healer, Alessandro Cagliostro.

It would take months for the trials of the arrested to commence and so in search of more news on the scandal a trade in gossip pamphlets began. These kinds of pamphlets were nothing new; indeed, just months after the diamond plotters' arrests, police apprehended one Pierre-Jacques Le Maitre, who'd spent years creating political pamphlets targeting the monarchy and governance. Throughout the 1770s, similar pamphlets had emerged mocking Marie Antoinette for her foreign birth, expensive tastes and alleged line of lovers. So, it was pretty easy for people to believe the new pamphlets on the Affair of the Diamond Necklace – Marie Antoinette was the woman behind the whole scheme. Her tastes were so extravagant and unbending that she'd colluded with prostitutes and pimps to spend the French people's money on a ridiculous folly. It cemented everything bad that had been rumoured, and by May 1786, the hatred towards the queen was so strong that she was unable to visit Notre Dame as the police simply couldn't protect her from the mob.

Finally, the trials commenced and though in court Marie Antoinette may have been exonerated, that was not the case in the court of public opinion. Although found guilty, Jeanne managed to escape prison and fled to London, where in 1789 she published a memoir, *Memoires Justificatifs de La Comtesse de Valois de La Motte*, which poured even more fuel on the fire. Jeanne painted Marie as a cold and calculating figure and

accused her of being a nymphomaniac as well as a closeted lesbian. The timing of this could not have been worse for the French royal family, with the Bastille falling that same July, and as the French Revolution swept the country, Jeanne's claims took root. Indeed, in the following months and years, the memory of the Affair of the Diamond Necklace led to a sea of pamphlets which portrayed the queen as both a greedy monster and wanton whore. Yet Jeanne would not return to see the ramifications of her scam play out, dying in 1791 while allegedly fleeing creditors. Marie Antoinette and her husband would die in 1793 at the hands of the revolutionaries. It was true that the king and queen spent frivolously while many of their people starved, but of the crime that solidified the vitriol against her, Marie Antoinette was in fact innocent.

Part IV

THE NINETEENTH CENTURY

THE TESTAMENT OF PETER THE GREAT

In recent years, the accomplishments of Russia's Peter the Great have been arguably mythologized and harkened back to Ivan III and Ivan the Terrible's dreams of '*gathering of the lands of Rus*' to promote and justify war and invasion. But this is far from the first time Peter the Great's history has been twisted to prop up totally disparate historical chapters. Indeed, there is a forgery of Peter the Great's will and testament, which is still taken as fact in some circles and has impacted global politics from the 1800s right up to today.

In 1812 French 'historian' and propagandist Charles Louis Lesur published the book *Des Progrès de la puissance russe depuis son origine jusqu'au commencement du XIX siècle* (*Of the Progress of Russian Power from Its Origin to the Nineteenth Century*). The book formed part of a campaign pushed forward by Napoleon Bonaparte to give grounds for France's invasion of Russia and included '*The Testament of Peter the Great*'. This was a fourteen-point plan towards the goal of Russia capturing all of Europe and conquering other countries such as Persia (now Iran), India and Turkey. The plan's purported steps included keeping Russia constantly at war, creating anarchy in Poland, turning countries against each other, and taking control of the Baltic and Black Seas. Lesur argued that although Peter the Great had died in 1725, he remained a threat to all of Europe. Credited with founding the Russian Empire and expanding its territory, Peter had in fact just been setting the stage for the task he would give to his successors – domination. France *had* to invade Russia; otherwise, Russia would take over first Europe and then, perhaps, the world. Lesur provided no proof that the Testament actually existed and there is no historic record of it before Lesur's 1812 claims. Still, this wasn't really looked into at the time because Lesur had done such a good job in creating something that would provoke potent levels of fear and mistrust.

Finally, in 1836, 'proof' of the discovery for the supposed Testament was given, albeit from a very strange source – French spy Le Chevalier d'Éon. The spy had died in 1810, and since then there had been a huge clamour for information on their life and death. The reason for this was that d'Éon had lived primarily as a woman, highly celebrated by early feminists as a symbol of what women could achieve. An autopsy after death showed that d'Éon had male genitalia, and although many historians now believe that d'Éon was likely transgender, this wasn't the point of view in 1836 – if a man had spent decades 'passing' as a woman, what other fantastical things might they have done. d'Éon's biography, *Memoires du Chevalier d'Éon*, written by Frédéric Gaillardet, provided the answer. It mixes the factual life of d'Éon with fictitious fantasy, tying in as many famous figures and events as possible to create exciting new affairs and escapades. One of these included d'Éon discovering the Testament of Peter the Great and sending it back to France in 1757. There is no evidence that this happened – no paper trail, no archived documents, no mention even by d'Éon in their own ghost-written 1779 biography. Yet it makes for a great story and, as we've already seen, sometimes that's enough to turn fiction into fact. It was certainly enough for the historian Walter Kelly, who included Gaillardet's version of events in his 1854 tome, *The History of Russia*. Interestingly, Kelly actually states that '*doubts have been cast upon both the memoirs and the so-called will*' and that the evidence supporting their claims had never '*undergone a thorough inquiry*' – yet he concludes that Russia's history around gathering its own Rus lands is enough evidence to mean that the Testament *must* be valid. In doing so, Kelly essentially cemented the Testament of Peter the Great in the annals of historic legend, and to this day both he and Gaillardet are the most cited sources for its legitimacy.

The Testament was next catapulted to the forefront of global politics following the outbreak of the Crimean War in 1853. Journalists were quick to include the Testament in their coverage of Russia's wartime actions, with Karl Marx and Friedrich Engels's writings in the *New York Tribune* arguably being the biggest instigators for this, claiming that the Testament guided all of Russia's foreign policy, proving '*the intrinsic barbarism of Russia herself*'. Panic around the supposed lasting machinations of Peter the Great was snowballing so fast that in 1859, thorough historical investigations finally began in earnest, and by the late 1870s, multiple findings concluded that the Testament was nothing but a forgery by Lesur.

PETER THE GREAT

Peter I or Peter the Great was crowned in 1682, first ruling alongside his half-brother, Ivan V, until 1696, when he became sole ruler after Ivan's death. Today, Peter is credited with modernizing Russia and consolidating its place within Europe.

Still, the use of the Testament never stopped; it's simply too good a propaganda tool. This was demonstrated by Germany during the First World War, targeting both France and Iran with new versions of the Testament in a bid to have them turn against Russia. The same tack was taken in the Second World War, although it now spread to all of Russia's European allies. Then in 1948, as the Cold War began to heat up, America's President Truman wrote that he feared no settlement could ever be made with the Soviet threat: *'they have fixed ideas and these ideas were set out by Peter the Great in his will – I suggest that you read it.'* In response, lawyer Grenville Clark sent a frantic all-caps note: '*IT WAS PUBLICIZED FOR PROPAGANDA PURPOSES SHORTLY BEFORE NAPOLEON'S INVASION OF RUSSIA AND IS APPARENTLY BEING USED FOR SIMILAR PURPOSES NOW.*' This didn't appear to make a difference, with several of Truman's aides later affirming that the president continued to at least privately speak of his belief in the Testament. And so it has continued, despite being debunked more than 150 years ago. Whenever Russia becomes engaged in war or invasion, you can be sure that the Testament of Peter the Great will once more emerge.

THE IMAGINARY WORLD OF GREGOR MACGREGOR

. . . .

While Lesur's forgery was rooting itself in European consciousness, another series of forgeries had led a group of pioneers to Nicaragua's Mosquito Coast. Eager to get their slice of the colonialism pie, they'd bought land in the hitherto unknown and unpopulated paradise of Poyais. Now on 10 September 1822, they were setting sail from London's dockside to start new lives and, hopefully, earn a fortune in the process. The only problem was that Poyais didn't exist and the settlers were about to find themselves trapped in the desolate wilds – their paradise lost.

Behind this disaster was one Gregor MacGregor. Born in Scotland in 1786, to a Captain of the East India Company, MacGregor spent much of his young adulthood mooching off family money and failing upwards. He'd bought himself a title in the British military, but by 1810 his inability to work well with others, and run-ins with higher-ups, led to his forced resignation. He began living off his wife's inherited wealth, but when she died suddenly in 1811, MacGregor was forced to find a job and he set his sights on becoming a mercenary. The Spanish American wars of independence had been underway since 1808. Macgregor was just one of many guns for hire who were happily welcomed by factions fighting for independence from Spain, partially triggered by the Napoleonic invasion of the Iberian Peninsula, but primarily from a deep-rooted and ever-growing discontent with Spanish authority. On arriving in Venezuela in 1813, MacGregor decided he didn't want to have to work his way up through the ranks and so created a fantastical CV for himself – he was now Sir Gregor, a storied hero of the British military. These claims dazzled so blindingly that it didn't take long for MacGregor to be fighting directly underneath Simón Bolívar aka El Libertador, in the Venezuelan War of Independence. Over the next few years, MacGregor excelled and by 1820 was conducting mercenary missions under the title of General of Division in the Army of Venezuela and New Granada.

It was while on a mission in the spring of 1820 that

MacGregor landed on the Mosquito Coast and learned of Poyais. The land was part of the Miskito Kingdom (more often referred to at the time as Mosquito) and had once been home to a British colony. However, in 1786, the British settlers were moved to the nearby colony of British Honduras, as part of a diplomatic agreement with Spain. Still, the Mosquito king and Britain had retained friendly relations; that was until 1814, when one George Arthur was appointed Lieutenant Governor of British Honduras. At the time Honduras was home to roughly 3,000 enslaved persons, many of whom had come from the Mosquito Shore, either being Miskitus who'd been sold into slavery or prisoners they'd sold on from raids on rival tribes. George Arthur had been shocked by the inhumane treatment of the slaves and was trying to arrange their freedom en masse, which didn't go down well with the slave owners or the Mosquito king. Seeing the way the tide was turning, the Mosquito king hoped to disentangle himself by finding new owners for parts of his land. When Gregor MacGregor came ashore, he seemed like just the ticket – totally oblivious to the ongoing turmoil and apparently uncaring of the fact that although Poyais may have once had rich verdant soil and the opportunity for a thriving timber trade, thanks to years of inaction, it was now pretty unhabitable.

Interestingly, in buying Poyais, Gregor MacGregor wasn't initially planning a long con. In this land, he hoped to build up a colony that could serve Latin American republican interests and also become a hub for British trade. He'd actually tried this tack a few years earlier in 1817, claiming the '*Republic of the Floridas*' in a Spanish island garrison just off the Florida coast. However, within three months of founding his new colony, a threatened attack by the Spanish caused him to flee and abandon the project altogether. In 1819, he'd tried again, this time attempting to seize Spanish ports near the Bay of Honduras and even crowning himself '*His Majesty the Inca of New Granada*'. Each time the Spanish would attack, MacGregor would make a run for it and he'd lose his new land. Poyais was his final shot at making this colony happen and at least this time he hadn't stolen the land.

When Gregor MacGregor returned to Britain in 1821, it was under the name the Cazique of Poyais. Knowing that Poyais, as it was, wouldn't be that tantalizing to buyers, he built up a marketing campaign around what Poyais *might* become in the distant future – crucially omitting the '*distant*' bit. Pamphlets, leaflets and maps were made to highlight the land's scenic mountain ranges, azure seas, and soil so fertile it could birth two crops in one season. One Captain Strangeways was paid to create a guidebook that emphasized the magnitude of the incredible timber fortunes just waiting to be amassed in Poyais. As MacGregor's sales efforts increased, so did the lies he was telling and the danger he was putting his new settlers in.

By 1822, the Poyais enterprise had grown enough to open offices in Edinburgh and London, giving the fledgling scam an air of legitimacy. That same year, financers jumped on board, awarding MacGregor a loan of £200,000 (roughly £27 million today). Budding colonists awaited MacGregor's word on when they could move into their new paradise, and never willing to let an opportunity slide, he obliged. A ship, the *Honduras Packet*, was acquired for the trip and MacGregor printed a new currency, having the colonists 'exchange' all their money for his bits of paper. With that, in September 1822, MacGregor cheerfully sent the colonists off to a barren wasteland.

The *Honduras Packet* landed in Poyais in early 1823 and as they began to unload the ship, a hurricane swept in. The ship's captain fled to avoid the worst of the weather, taking most of the supplies with him and leaving the settlers marooned with little to survive. The situation quickly escalated, when on 22 March, a second shipload of colonists arrived. Once again, the captain swiftly left, and now almost 250 people were trapped in Poyais. None of them had been prepared for what awaited them and their crude attempts to survive kept failing. The seeds they planted withered and died; their tents and makeshift huts couldn't stand up to the weather; and without proper sanitation, disease swept their camps. Luckily, between the survivors and the Miskitus, word of the castaways had reached British Honduras and in May a rescue mission was mounted. Of those that survived their colonial adventure, most settled in Belize with some returning to Britain. Two more ships stuffed with MacGregor's colonists arrived in 1823 but thankfully, on seeing the desolation that awaited, they turned back or were halted at Belize.

STRANGE BUT TRUE

In examining MacGregor's outlandish scheme, many historians originally thought that the guidebook by Captain Strangeways had to be a fake, written by MacGregor. However, there was actually a Captain Thomas Strangeways who was a former officer of the 65th Regiment once stationed in the British West Indies — why he agreed to play into the scheme, we don't know.

Meanwhile, Gregor MacGregor was nowhere to be found. As news of the Poyais disaster spread, he'd fled Britain. However, he would reappear two years later in France, where he was once more setting up offices to sell his Poyais land, this time promising that the area was rich in gold. Somehow, he found success in the scheme, securing settlers and even landing a loan of £300,000. Fortunately, just before his French ships could set sail, the authorities caught up with him and by the end of 1825, MacGregor was facing fraud charges. For unknown reasons, these charges were dropped and in 1827, the conman made the strange decision to return to the scene of the crime in Britain to try the scheme again. Almost immediately, he was arrested for fraud, but again the charges were dropped. After this close call, MacGregor appears to have called time on his illicit schemes, living off his ill-gotten gains until he returned to Venezuela in 1839. There he was granted the return of his title as Division General and was given a sizeable pension. Gregor MacGregor died in 1845 in Caracas, his obituaries lauding him as a '*hero*'.

THE GREAT MOON HOAX

On 25 August 1835, residents of New York woke up to the startling news that British astronomer Sir John Herschel had found life on the Moon. Not just any life, but a whole society of sophisticated beings who'd built mammoth monuments alongside ecological systems to benefit from the Moon's plentiful rivers and forests. This landmark discovery was reported by the *New York Sun*, from an extract it had acquired from that month's copy of the *Edinburgh Journal of Science*, and not wanting to leave its readers in the lurch after learning of such an important scientific find, the *Sun* promised more information in the next day's edition. It would more than deliver on this, soon imparting news of the Moon being infested by man-bats who flew far above its surface, as well as herds of unicorns and beavers that appeared part human.

A frenzy broke out, with copies of the *New York Sun* selling out so quickly that their offices were besieged by eager readers desperate to lay their hands on the latest edition. They were joined by a group of scientists from Yale University, who were keen to speak to the team at the *Edinburgh Journal of Science*. Not knowing what to do about this, the *Sun*'s staff sent the scientists on a wild goose chase around New York until they eventually gave up and returned to Yale. Sir John Herschel, who was on an expedition in South Africa, didn't find out about the fervour around his discovery until a few days later, and when he did, he was confused as he'd never conducted such research. The editors and writers of the *Edinburgh Journal of Science* were equally perplexed, mainly because the journal had shut down three years earlier. It didn't take long for the public at large to realize they'd been duped – honestly, doubts had started to creep in once man-bats were introduced to the fray.

The British press were quick to mock America for believing such tripe, despite multiple international newspapers, including some in Britain, picking up the *Sun*'s pieces and publishing them as fact, long after the hoax had been rumbled. London's *Herald* declared that Americans were addicted to excitement: '*When no excitement exists, it must be created in some way or other, for to an American it is a sort of intellectual food.*' Yet it wasn't an American who'd made up the hoax, it was the *New York Sun*'s British-born editor, Richard Adams Locke.

Prior to the Moon hoax making its way onto the pages of the paper, the *Sun*'s readership was at roughly 8,000; after they broke the news of Herschel's 'find' it was around 19,360, making the *Sun* – for a brief period – one of America's most read newspapers. The whole thing had been an elaborate ploy to gain readers and it had worked; even after the hoax was discovered, the newspaper didn't face much fallout – for the readers it had been a fun ride while it lasted. Herschel himself laughed it off, calling it '*a very clever piece of imagination*'. The only real lasting damage was the anger of young writer Edgar Allan Poe, who accused the *Sun* of stealing his story 'The Unparalleled Adventure of One Hans Pfaall', which had been published two months before the Moon hoax. Interestingly, Poe wasn't enraged merely because Locke had plagiarized his work, but because he was hoping Hans Pfaall itself would be a long-running satirical hoax.

To that point, these kinds of grand public hoaxes had been

the realm of writers or random participants. Individuals like Mary Toft or authors such as Monmouth and Mandeville. As science ramped up in the 1700s, so did the work of writers who were inspired by its findings to create fantastical fiction and, like Poe, if you were able to pass off your stories as fact – at least for a time – your readership would boom. The *New York Sun* had thrown all of that out of the window and in doing so created a new genre – fake news. It was picked up by newspapers as an easy way to fill out slow news days and sell more papers. Edgar Allan Poe even let go of his anger at Locke, once he was bought in to create some fake news of his own, 1844's Balloon hoax.

THE REAL JOHN HERSCHEL

Although he didn't discover life on the Moon, Sir John Herschel did name several of the moons of Saturn and Uranus as well as discovering multiple galaxies. He is also credited with establishing the use of the Julian day system in astronomy and his 1831 work, *A Preliminary Discourse on the Study of Natural Philosophy*, would inspire Charles Darwin.

As the 1800s rolled on, so did the craze for fake news. Much of this was pretty silly stuff, such as 1895's Maggie Murphy hoax, which involved a man carrying a giant potato. One man's work, however, stands out, that of fledgling journalist

Samuel Langhorne Clemens, later known as Mark Twain. In 1862, he dipped his toe in the waters of fake news with an article about a petrified man that had become a tourist attraction in a Californian mountain range. However, as more journalists indulged in the falsifying of news, the bar for their lies crept higher. Twain took this to an early extreme in 1863, writing in the *Territorial Enterprise* about a man called John Hopkins who'd murdered his wife and children, after going mad from losing his investments in San Francisco utilities. Hopkins didn't exist and fortunately nor did his family, but in creating this macabre news, Twain wanted to not only grab his audience's attention but show them the failings he saw in the utility companies' practices. For this stunt, Twain almost lost his job, but a precedent was being set. Gone were the days of unicorns and man-bats, fake news was about to enter a very dangerous era.

ABRAHAM LINCOLN AND THE INVENTION OF MISCEGENATION

Abolition was the word of the moment in the run-up to 1864's American presidential election. Taking place in the midst of the Civil War, with Confederate states abstaining completely, in the minds of most politicians the focus of the election should have been on the future of the Union – to continue the war or broker peace. But the question of emancipation was inescapable.

The Democratic nominee, George B. McClellan, viewed slavery as an institution protected by constitutional rights, so when he advocated a wholesale re-establishment of the Union with the offer that any Confederate state that rejoined would be *'received at once with a full guarantee of all its constitutional rights'*, he was essentially saying that under his presidency, no state would be forced to free its slaves. In the other corner was the Republican nominee and current president, Abraham Lincoln. Since his first term as president, Lincoln had been bound up in the abolition issue. In 1861 and 1862, he'd tried and failed with schemes to buy out slave owners, ultimately leading to 1863's Emancipation Proclamation. This made it law that all slaves held within 'rebel' states *'are, and henceforth shall be freed'*. Of course, they'd only *actually* be freed if the Union won, but Lincoln had made his position clear, and following the proclamation, an estimated 200,000 slaves managed to run away under its promises of freedom.

A vote for Lincoln then would be a vote for the complete abolishment of slavery. This caused dissent within the Republican Party itself, as many of the wealthy would lose billions in the form of human capital if emancipation went ahead, not to mention the fear that abolition would just lead to even more war. Then there was the so-called Copperhead press, newspapers that were largely aligned with a peace arm of the Democratic Party, which blamed abolition for the war. Most of this type of press popped up around the time of the Emancipation Proclamation, and they busied themselves in creating stories that used often imaginary pseudo-science to prove black people were inferior or promote news (real and fake) that could be skewed to paint America's black population as 'barbarians' and 'monsters'. However, what these newspapers were most successful in was the tactic of scaremongering – that emancipation would lead to so-called '*negro supremacy*'. For example, in July 1863, Copperhead paper *The Age* used commendations given to the 1st Kansas Colored Infantry Regiment to argue: '*This we suppose is another confirmation of the truth of the abolition doctrine that a negro is as good as a white man! ... The worship of the "ebony idol" is still to go on, whilst the interest of millions of free white men are to be entirely ignored in this cruel war for the "African" and his race.*'

Two newsmen, David Goodman Croly and George Wakeman, realized that to truly prevent emancipation, confining their cause to the Copperhead press wasn't enough. They needed to target abolitionists. Croly was the managing editor of the *World*, a New York Copperhead leaning paper, while Wakeman was a reporter there, and in 1863 both men began writing a pamphlet entitled *Miscegenation: The Theory of Blending of the Races*. The 'anonymous' author cites that science had shown that black American men were the '*ideal of true manhood*' and that the future of humanity depended on interracial marriage, as '*miscegenetic or mixed races are much superior, mentally, physically, and morally, to those pure or unmixed.*' Such ideas were deliberately revolutionary in nature. Even within abolitionist groups, the notion of interracial marriage was taboo, to the extent that Croly and Wakeman ended up inventing a word to describe their faux-scientific concept of mixed-race relationships – miscegenation.

It should also be noted that neither Croly nor Wakeman actually believed in any of what they were writing; indeed, quite the opposite, they thought that white people were inherently superior. Their pamphlet was all part of an elaborate scheme. They'd infiltrate the abolitionists, coax them into signing off on the incendiary pamphlet, and then use their own newspaper to spread fear of this.

By Christmas 1863, *Miscegenation* had begun to arrive on the doorsteps of the leaders of the abolitionist movement. Two months later, in February, it was published, available at newsstands, and advertised heavily in the pro-abolition press. Quickly, this new-fangled theory of 'miscegenation' was a hot-button issue, even being debated in the House of Representatives. Rumours swirled that under Lincoln forced miscegenation would become law – that this had been the true plan of emancipation all along. Croly and Wakeman happily exacerbated their self-spawned mess, writing in the *World*: *'If marriage is recommended for a white man with a black woman begetting his children – then precisely the same solution might be asked in relation to incest, or any other abomination which the progressists have not yet dubbed with a euphemistic name.'*

Miscegenation was now a fully fledged campaign issue. As the election approached in September 1864, some anti-abolitionists appeared to be trying to tempt an all-out race war. A year earlier in July, a contingent of New York's white Irish immigrant community had begun to attack black citizens, resulting in a massacre that totalled around 120 deaths. In writing *Miscegenation*, Croly and Wakeman had seized on this, at one point stating: *'The fusion between Negro and Irish will be of infinite service to the Irish. They are a more brutal race and lower in civilization than the Negro ... Of course, we speak of the laboring Irish.'* Now, pamphlets plastered with this quote were circling New York. To fuel this further, the *World* published a supposedly satirical story, accompanied by cartoons, that the city had just held a 'Miscegenation Ball' in honour of Lincoln.

MARK TWAIN'S MISCEGENATION

In May 1864, determined not to be outdone as the de facto king of journalistic hoaxes, Mark Twain published his own version of the Miscegenation hoax, in which he claimed that funds collected for Union soldiers were being diverted to *'aid a Miscegenation Society somewhere in the East'*. Twain later apologized for the fake news, saying he'd written it whilst drunk. However, this and his other questionable journalistic tactics led to calls for a duel, upon which Twain fled to San Francisco.

This was read by many as a factual event, where *'one hundred and fifty coal-black wenches'* danced with Republican politicians, the author noting: *'the smell was so strong it set us sneezing, so we started away from the Miscegen Ball.'*

Ultimately, the efforts of Croly and Wakeman would fail, in that Lincoln was elected president in 1864. Two weeks after Lincoln returned to the White House, the *World* 'exposed' miscegenation as a hoax, of course not naming Croly or Wakeman, although noting: *'the wicked wags, its authors, left events to their natural course; and from their anonymous castle of safety watched with delight the almost divine honors paid to their Abbot of Misrul.'* The whole thing was passed off as a harmless prank by two cheeky scamps and as such the news of their elaborate lie remained relatively localized, not interesting enough to be picked up by other American newspapers. So the theory of miscegenation and the fear surrounding it continued in the public consciousness. In the following decades, multiple states enacted Miscegenation Laws, legally banning interracial marriage. In 1883, the US Supreme Court ruled that such laws didn't break any part of the constitution and it wouldn't be until 1964 that American law started to lay the groundwork to reverse this move and prevent states from banning interracial marriage. Croly and Wakeman may not have bought down Lincoln, but they got away with something just as massive, leading to more than a century's worth of suffering, division and lost love.

THE GREATEST CONMAN

One of the few public debunkings of miscegenation actually came from P. T. Barnum, who in his 1865 book, *Humbugs of the World*, applauded the hoax, revelling in how it successfully fooled so many whilst spreading ideology that encouraged separating people by race. This might be a surprising take by the famed showman, whose recent appearances in pop culture have shown him to be a warm man, who bridged the gap between human differences. However, behind that glittery façade lies something far darker and more historically damaging.

Born in 1810, Phineas Taylor Barnum had tried and failed in several business ventures before he stumbled across the world of showmanship in 1835. Word had spread of a sideshow attraction in Philadelphia, dubbed *'the Greatest Natural and National Curiosity in the World!'* This curiosity was a black woman named Joice Heth, who was touted as over 160 years old and the former 'mammy' to George Washington. Joice was owned by one R. W. Lindsay, who was keen to sell off his attraction and return home to Kentucky. Barnum swept in, bought Joice for $1,000, and immediately set off with her on a tour of the north-eastern United States. Shows began with a reading of Joice's bill of sale before the elderly woman was paraded in front of crowds and asked to recall her memories of *'dear little George'*. Barnum of course knew that Joice wasn't actually 161 years old, but she was very frail, so much so that ticket sales began to dry up once the tour exhausted the woman enough that she could do little more than sit on the stage. To drum up interest, Barnum began to leak stories to the press that Joice was in fact an automaton, as well as accounts of everything from her smell (of tobacco) and her bowel movements (once in a fortnight). When Boston's *Courier* newspaper decried Barnum's treatment of Joice, stating, *'Humanity sickens at the exhibition'*, the showman was quick to cover his back, creating a pamphlet filled with lurid and likely false claims of the horrific treatment Joice had received at the hands of other slave masters – Barnum might own Joice but he wasn't technically torturing her, was he?

In February 1836, Joice died, yet her death wouldn't prevent Barnum from making money. A public autopsy was arranged, with over 1,500 people paying 50 cents each to watch the old woman be cut up. The autopsy found that Joice was not the oldest woman in America, but in her eighties, which set off a media feeding frenzy. Newspapers like the *New York Sun* excitedly recounted the autopsy in vivid detail, while Barnum told the *New York Herald* that the woman autopsied had actually not been Joice, who was alive and well, but '*a respectable old negress called Aunt Nelly*'. Joice's death and the hoaxes around it proved to be the making of Barnum. He'd created a pop culture spectacle, and both the public and the press couldn't wait to see what he'd do next.

His next major foray was Barnum's Grand Scientific and Musical Theater, touting circus acts and human 'curiosities'. From Joice Heth, Barnum had learned what he saw as the art of the '*humbug*'. In his words, the audience '*appears disposed to be amused even when they are conscious of being deceived*'. In 1841, the theatre was turned into a permanent attraction in New York, Barnum's American Museum. Stuffed to the brim with '*a million wonders*', which included exhibits that Barnum himself created, most famously, the FeeJee Mermaid. This consisted of the head and partial body of a monkey that had been sewn onto a fish and was an oddity that had been passed back and forth between sea captains before landing in the lap of Barnum in 1842. Aware that nobody would actually believe him if he said this was a mermaid, Barnum conducted a bizarre hoax. He sent letters to American newspapers mentioning that a '*Dr. Griffin of the Lyceum of Natural History in London*' had uncovered a mermaid and would be coming with it to America. Then Barnum had his lawyer, Levi Lyman, pose as Dr Griffin, check into a Philadelphia hotel, and 'accidentally' show the mermaid to its landlord, who immediately went to the press. 'Griffin' then travelled to New York, where he met reporters and 'sold' the mermaid to Barnum for display.

Strange amalgamated creatures aside, the museum's biggest draw was its living exhibits. These included Charles Stratton, a child with dwarfism who Barnum essentially bought from his parents at the age of five; Salvadorian siblings Maximo and Bartola, who had developmental disabilities and were restyled as '*the Aztec Wonders*'; and '*Siamese twins*' Chang and Eng Bunker. Perhaps the most famous of Barnum's living curiosities was William Henry Johnson, a young black man from New Jersey who had microcephaly and worked as a cook. In 1859, Charles Darwin released his groundbreaking work, *The Origin of Species*, and hoping to capitalize on the insatiable interest in Darwin's theories, Barnum exhibited William as the missing link, dubbing him '*what is it*', and claiming the young man was found in Africa. A mammoth marketing campaign was started, with advertisements blaring: '*WHAT IS IT? Is it a lower order of MAN? Or is it a higher order of MONKEY? None can tell!*'

It has been argued that although Barnum's 'curiosities'

THE 'GREAT' MUSEUM

Barnum's American Museum at first hosted collections that included stuffed animals, wax figures and 'ancient artifacts of the orient'. As time went on, Barnum built an aquarium, gardens and even a zoo on the upper floors, with lions, tigers and bears. In 1861, this menagerie expanded to include beluga whales, who were kept in a tank in the museum's basement.

---

were treated like animals in a human zoo, many were paid and offered opportunities they may not have otherwise had. This is certainly true in some cases. Charles Stratton, for one, became independently wealthy and a later business partner of Barnum. Others weren't so lucky, particularly those with more severe disabilities; for example, Maximo and Bartola continued to be sold from showman to showman, and despite being siblings were made to marry each other in an 1867 publicity stunt. But the problems with Barnum's human zoo went far beyond those made to inhabit it. At a time when America was forced to negotiate its own diversity, Barnum was making wild claims and presenting them as truth. Visitors to the museum were shown the '*barbarous*' roots of minority groups. Just within the singular case of *What Is It*, Barnum spun a tale of adventurers, who while hunting gorillas along the River Gambia, stumbled across the man in front of them. A pamphlet purporting to delve into the science behind this '*discovery*' stated that the man had been examined '*by some of the most scientific men we have and pronounced by them to be a connecting link between the wild African native and the brute creation*'. William Henry Johnson wasn't just a guy from Jersey, wearing a costume and being told to act '*backward*', he was a horrifying symbol of otherness.

Interestingly, in 1864, Barnum entered the political sphere and appeared to have shifted his views, standing against slavery and in one speech admitting: '*I whipped my slaves. I ought to have been whipped a thousand times for this myself.*' Partially thanks to his heavily publicized abolitionist viewpoints, in 1865, he was elected the Republican Representative for Fairfield, Connecticut. That same year, Barnum's American Museum burned down, and though it was replaced, that museum too would catch fire in 1868. Following this, Barnum moved into the circus game, while still concentrating on his political ambitions. In 1869, he *almost* apologized for his treatment of Joice Heth, admitting that he now knew owning a person to be wrong, but blamed Joice entirely for the scheme itself. How much of Barnum's turnaround was for show is unknown. He certainly put on the appearance of a stand-up Republican, promoting evangelicalism and teetotal values. But tellingly, during an 1883 raid of New York's brothels, at least one was found to be under the tenancy of Barnum himself. It appears more likely then that Barnum was indeed the greatest showman, happy to lie and bend however best to make a profit.

BISMARCK AND THE ART OF WAR

In the mid-1800s, the star of the Germanic kingdom and state, Prussia was on the rise, almost transforming its place on the world stage in little more than half a century. An industrial powerhouse, its steel and coal industries could equal those of European heavyweights, and as its plucky population crept up, so did the threat that if Prussia could unite the majority of German Confederation states under its umbrella, it might become one of, if not *the* most powerful state in Europe. Of course, that didn't stop the continent's big boys from bullying it. Though half of Prussia was an industrial might, half was rural, entrenched in provincial traditions and religion, mercilessly mocked as a place of peasantry and outdated belief. Prussia may have been tipped for success, but for many countries, it was kind of a joke, as Britain's *The Times* newspaper said in 1860: '*How* [it] *became a great power history tells us, why she remains so, nobody can tell.*'

Otto von Bismarck was determined to change this. He was born in 1815, the year the Napoleonic Wars ended and the German Confederation was created. This group of German-speaking states was a mixed bag to say the least; some states like Austria and Prussia far outstripped others in terms of population, industry and economy and as such were often the ones holding most of the power. It was a pretty broken system, ineffective in terms of both economy and might. Bismarck had seen all of this first hand; thanks to his family's wealth, he'd spent much of his youth drifting around Prussia and Germany, occasionally trying his hand at jobs but mostly just hanging out and chasing girls. However, in 1847, he fell into politics, and it quickly became apparent that his natural charisma and ability to read any person made him more than just a good party guest – he was a born politician. Bismarck quickly rose through the ranks, known for his intelligence, eloquence and extremely impulsive nature.

By 1862, Bismarck was Minister President of Prussia and had formed an idea of what the state needed to do to secure its dominance – get rid of the blustering confederation and unify Germany. This was a very big plan and one that would be incredibly hard to carry off. Following uprisings against the confederation in 1848 and 1849, there had been an attempt to unify the country; however, it ultimately failed. Part of the reason for this was how staunchly Austria was against it – a unified Germany posed a threat to the Austrian Empire as a whole, not to mention that unification would give Prussia more power. In fact, once it had been agreed to throw out the push for unification, in 1850, Austria had Prussia promise to never attempt to unify the country again and to not challenge Austrian rule. If Bismarck carried out his plan, Austria was sure to come down hard on Prussia – but only if Austria was still in the picture.

Bismarck decided that the best course of action was to go to war with Austria. The problem was that not many people in Prussia wanted a war, particularly one against their old ally

Austria. So, Bismarck engineered one. When Prussia's Landtag refused his request to expand the army, he went behind their backs and did some creative financial planning, privatizing assets and falsifying tax receipts to get the military money he needed. In 1865, he secretly met with the French leader, Napoleon III, and managed to get him to agree to have Prussia's back if a war broke out, despite only ever alluding to promises of gifts of land in return. Finally, in 1866, Bismarck created yet another secret alliance, this time with Italy. Then he embarked on a campaign of annoying Austria to the point of war, making outlandish demands, from Prussia taking over swathes of the confederation to declaring that the confederation itself had to be dissolved for an elected parliament. By June, war had broken out. Between Italy and Prussia, it didn't take long for a victory to be secured, the Austro-Prussian War only lasting a little over a month. Austria licked its wounds and turned its attention away from Germany, while Bismarck happily oversaw the unification of the country's northern states into one new coalition.

Prussia had proved itself and upended European politics; in the space of a month it had added millions of people to its population and its territory was now far vaster. Gone was the butt of Europe's jokes, in its place, a powerful threat. France was more than aware of this and during the Austro-Prussian War, several advisers of Napoleon III had advocated that France should '*Smash Prussia and take the Rhine*'. But Napoleon was reticent; instead, he opted to ask Bismarck to return the Borders of 1814, referring to a large stretch of Germany that had been once annexed by France but returned to Germany following the Battle of Waterloo. Bismarck was never going to do this – after all, it wouldn't earn him much favour at home. Still, he had to do something to appease France and went for the bare minimum, giving independence in name alone to a few French-aligned states. Unsurprisingly, this didn't go down well in France – the whole Prussian affair was proving a monumental embarrassment to Napoleon. This only got worse as Prussia continued to flourish and Napoleon's reputation took beating after beating. As tensions grew, it became clear that it wasn't a matter of if there would be a war, but when.

Bismarck was very open to this. He had the northern states of Germany, but he wanted it all and if he'd learned one thing, it was that the states tended to unite behind a banner of patriotic pride during times of war. If he played this right, not only would Prussia defeat a global superpower, but he'd finally be able to unify the country for good. So Bismarck tried to do the same thing he'd done with Austria – goad France into war – and although it almost broke out in 1867, 1868 and 1869, nothing really took off. Bismarck was getting desperate, and then the Spanish Parliament approached Prussian Prince Leopold with the offer to become the new royal house and take the throne. Neither Leopold nor Prussian King Wilhelm I wanted this, as it was far too likely that Leopold would quickly lose the throne. But Bismarck saw an opportunity – Leopold landing the Spanish throne would enrage not only Napoleon but Napoleon's Spanish wife, Eugénie. He was right, the French were angry, but still, they didn't start the war. Instead, they sent their Prussian Ambassador, Count Vincent

THE LAST EMPEROR

Napoleon III would be the last Emperor of France. He seized power in a coup d'état in 1851, but by the time of his run-in with Bismarck, things were falling apart. His final blow came during the Franco-Prussian War's Battle of Sedan, fought between 1 and 2 September 1870. Napoleon III ordered his troops to surrender and was captured and held prisoner. On 19 September, Bismarck's troops besieged Paris, a blockade which would last until an armistice was agreed on 26 January 1871. By the 28th, the war was won. Napoleon III would be deposed and exiled.

Benedetti, to try to talk sense into Wilhelm I as he holidayed in the town of Bad Ems.

Yet this wouldn't be necessary, as out of the blue, on 12 July 1870, Leopold withdrew his candidacy for the throne. Back in Ems, Wilhelm I was delighted with his cousin's decision and on seeing Benedetti, he applauded a peaceful end to the crisis. Benedetti agreed but passed on that France would like Prussia to publicly promise to never attempt to take the Spanish throne again. The mood somewhat ruined, Wilhelm tipped his hat and left without a word. Back in Germany, Bismarck was frustratedly planning his next move after yet another attempt at war had been scuppered. Then a telegrammed report of

Wilhelm and Benedetti's meeting landed on his lap. It was pretty innocuous – the two men had met, it had been polite if awkward – that was it. Yet in this small exchange, Bismarck saw an opportunity. He forged a new version of events, one in which Benedetti confronted Wilhelm, demanding that Prussia back down; a furious Wilhelm had spurned him, storming off and refusing to talk to the French Ambassador again. Bismarck then put this lie into a press release and sent it out far and wide. By 13 July, France's alleged rudeness and Prussia's belittling of its ambassador was international news. Enraged and embarrassed, Napoleon rallied his troops and on 19 July, he declared war. Ultimately, the Franco-Prussian War would last just over six months, with Bismarck and Prussia emerging victorious. Bismarck's plan worked, and the war did lead to German unification, creating a new European superpower. Otto von Bismarck had quite literally forged his way to an empire.

THE USS *MAINE* AND THE WAR OF WORDS

'You furnish the pictures, and I'll furnish the war' – In 1897, young newspaper magnate William Randolph Hearst supposedly said this to the American painter Frederic Remington. The artist had been hired by Hearst to go to Cuba and depict the outbreak of the Spanish–American War. The only problem

was that no war had broken out and in Remington's opinion it never would – he wanted to go home. Hearst's refusal and adamance that with or without a real war he could make one happen in print has gone down in history, evidence of the might of the media. Now, Hearst probably didn't actually ever say this, or at least there's no concrete evidence that he did. However, that's not to say there's no grain of truth in this misquote, or that it doesn't indicate the lies Hearst *was* willing to tell to make this war sell newspapers.

In the 1890s, the term 'yellow journalism' was gaining traction. Gone were the days of wholly fictitious news such as the Great Moon Hoax or Mark Twain's fantastical familial murder spree; now, newspapers were merely bending facts to create sensational stories that supported their own biases. Despite the new name, realistically, yellow journalism was the same as what had come before, just toned down. So much so in fact that one of the leading yellow journalism papers *was* the *New York World*, which only a few decades earlier had been behind the miscegenation scandal. Now rebranded, the *World* was run by Joseph Pulitzer and had become known as a hub for buzzy scandalous news. Its offices towered above those of other New York newspapers and Pulitzer's ploys for his paper's publicity were splashed across not only the *World*, but internationally too. That was until 1895, when Hearst bought the failing *New York Journal* and began not only poaching Pulitzer's staff, but also competing for circulation. The two newspapers became locked in a battle for readers, both men determined to succeed, seeing the win as the next step in creating their own media empires.

Neck and neck, the pair pinned their hopes on the growing hostilities between Spain and the United States – whoever won this war of words would be the ultimate victor.

In 1895, Cuba began a fight for its independence from Spain. With the island country so close to its borders, the American public took great interest in the war of independence, and both the *Journal* and *World* were more than happy to play into this, often siding with the Cuban rebels and reporting on both true and false Spanish atrocities against them. The journalistic standards of both newspapers were frequently non-existent; for example, in 1898, *Journal* reporter James Creelman actively joined in a battle against Spanish troops in El Caney, claiming their flag in the name of his newspaper and getting shot in the process. Another *Journal* correspondent, Richard Harding Davis, almost caused an international incident when in 1897 he falsely accused Spanish officials of publicly stripping and humiliating women on board an American ship. The Spanish outrage at this lie reached the House of Representatives and was only quelled when the *World* smugly outed Davis's report as fraudulent.

Despite the fallout these false articles could bring, they raked in hundreds of thousands, if not at times, over a million readers – but the newspaper owners wanted more. In 1897, Hearst orchestrated an international campaign around a beautiful young woman named Evangelina Cisneros, who'd been imprisoned by the Spanish along with her Cuban rebel father. Suggesting Evangelina had actually been arrested after fighting off a Spanish officer's rape attempt, Hearst drafted in support from high-profile women including the president's own mother, before having one of his reporters dramatically break Evangelina out of jail, heralding the break-out as '*what could not be accomplished by petition and urgent request of the Pope ...* [Spain] *could not build a jail that would hold against* Journal *enterprise when properly set to work.*' The humanitarian publicity stunt was huge news, boosting the *Journal*'s sales and furthering public agreement that the US should intervene in Cuba's War of Independence. Still, the American military wasn't budging. If Hearst and Pulitzer wanted record sales, they'd need to find a bigger story to push the country into war.

The USS *Maine* was sent to Havana Harbor in January 1898 to oversee and protect US interests, partially in response to the outcry generated by Hearst and Pulitzer. On the night of 15 February, an accidental explosion on board the ship caused it to sink, killing 266 men. Within minutes of the explosion, a *World* reporter based in Havana sent a wired telegram to the newspaper headquarters, and an hour later the *World* had arranged for a team of divers to explore the wreckage. Unfortunately for Pulitzer, his divers' tugboat was turned away by the Spanish authorities; however, the *Journal* somehow managed to get its own divers into the wreckage, allegedly before the US Navy had mustered its own investigative diving team. By 17 February, the *Journal* was excitedly reporting: '*The* Maine *was destroyed by a torpedo. It makes clear that the destruction of the* Maine *was not brought about by an accidental explosion ... it is very clear that a Spanish fanatic or a secret emissary of the Spanish Government floated the torpedo under the waterline against the* Maine's *forward magazine and set it with a detonating device, giving him time to escape.'* The *Journal* didn't actually know this to be the case, as its diving team hadn't been prepared to investigate properly. Instead, they'd just been thrown into the harbour so they could be the first on the scene. The investigation, in turn, had been short, unthorough and hampered by how horrifically traumatized the team was by what they'd witnessed, with the sailors' bodies still in the water. These reports were combined with leaks from government divers who'd had to call off their own initial search early due to poor visibility in the water. The *Journal* didn't know it was clearly a torpedo because they had no concrete facts, but they printed anyway, turning a possible cause into fact and declaring that Spain had attacked America.

As the US continued its official investigation, the *Journal* and *World* continued the campaign of essentially making up the news. Hearst offered a $50,000 reward for information on the culprit of the *Maine* disaster, while the *World* announced it was Spanish *'terrorism'* and released diagrams of all the ways a single boat could have attacked the warship. By the 21st, it was being reported that war with Spain was imminent, backed up with lurid illustrations of drowned sailors and interviews with grieving families. With both newspapers offering the most content in terms of articles and illustrations, their reporting was picked up by American and international press, with the angle of *'Spain bombs innocent sailors'* becoming the fixed narrative. In March, the US Navy released its findings, which concluded that the evidence found by divers was not enough to truly substantiate events; however, the most likely cause of the explosion was that the *Maine* had accidentally hit a mine, which had triggered the explosion of the ship's forward magazines. Crucially, it was unknown whose mine it was – it could have been new or it could have been present in the harbour for a long time.

THE PULITZER

Joseph Pulitzer struggled for the rest of his life to come to terms with his role in the *Maine* frenzy and its abandoning of journalistic ethics. Perhaps in an effort to make good, Joseph Pulitzer requested in his will that an award be made in his name to incentivize excellence and public service in journalism, which became known as the Pulitzer Prize. Since its inception in 1917, the Pulitzer Prize has been expanded, so it now also includes awards in other fields including poetry, music and photography.

The report remained under wraps as it wound its way through Congress, and while waiting for the final verdict, the *Journal* and *World* went back to theorizing everything from a huge Spanish conspiracy to Spanish mines. Throughout March, President McKinley delayed releasing the report to the public, as he wanted to try to end the Cuban War of Independence through diplomacy, avoiding any further bloodshed. However, the actions of the yellow press had increased public pressure for America to go to war, and if the government handed the

Maine report to the press, they'd almost certainly turn a mine of unknown origin into a Spanish mine – making war inevitable. However, pressure from Congress meant that the report had to be released. On 25 March, the *Journal* front page read: '*SPAIN GUILTY! Destroyed with a floating mine!*'. The public outcry was immediate – '*Remember the* Maine! *To hell with Spain!*' – and most Americans couldn't understand why their president was allowing such an attack to pass without ramifications. As tensions between the nations heated up, McKinley issued a demand for Spain to allow Cuba its freedom; in return, Spain abandoned negotiations and the US Navy formed a blockade. On 23 April, Spain declared war, with America following on 25 April. Ultimately America would win out, gaining control of Cuba, Puerto Rico and Guam.

THE DREYFUS AFFAIR

'*J'accuse!*' – This phrase would become a nationwide fascination and cause of major division, but on 13 January 1898, it was one headline, emblazoned on the front page of the French newspaper *L'Aurore*. In an explosive open letter by the novelist Émile Zola, the French military and government were accused of wrongly imprisoning one Alfred Dreyfus, of falsifying evidence, and knowingly spreading anti-Semitic ideology. These were enormous claims and would open the floodgates not only to an investigation but set forth a truly world-changing series of events.

The man in the middle of all of this was decidedly average. Born in 1859 in Alsace–Lorraine, Alfred Dreyfus was the youngest child in a large Jewish family. Following the Franco-Prussian war, his family was forced to leave Alsace–Lorraine after it was annexed by Germany. Because of this experience of war, Dreyfus joined the French Army as soon as he could, and thanks to his whip-smart intelligence, he was cherry-picked to attend some of the military's most lofty training programmes. By 1892, the now Captain Dreyfus was awarded a place as an intern within the General Staff. Still, despite the accolades, Dreyfus was frequently ostracized due to his Jewish heritage and faith. Jewish officers were a tiny minority within the army, with only around 300 serving at the same time as Dreyfus, yet their presence had become incredibly controversial.

Throughout the 1880s, much of Europe had experienced a growth in anti-Semitic feeling, partly due to high-profile international news stories, such as a blood libel case in Austria–

Hungary (known as the Tiszaeszlár affair) that revived a conspiracy frenzy similar to that of the Simon of Trent case in the 1400s. Concurrent to this were a series of pogroms that swept Russia, alongside Tsar Alexander III implementing laws to stamp out Jewish citizens' rights. What Dreyfus and his fellow Jewish soldiers were experiencing was just the tip of the iceberg, but it was very real, with violence towards the soldiers a regular occurrence.

It was in this climate of misjudged fear and distrust that France found they had a rat in their ranks. In the late summer of 1894, a letter was uncovered that showed someone within the French military had been leaking information to the German military attaché, Maximilian von Schwartzkoppen. A frantic investigation to find the traitor commenced and very quickly the blame was pinned on Alfred Dreyfus. His role in the General Office meant he may have had access to information; he came from Alsace–Lorraine, which was now part of Germany, and he was Jewish, so shouldn't be trusted – that was the evidence, but it was all they needed. Though Dreyfus maintained his innocence, he was found guilty of treason and sentenced to life imprisonment on Devil's Island. The news of his arrest and trial was front-page stuff, and when in January 1895 Dreyfus was publicly stripped of his military titles, it was watched by a crowd of some 20,000 who cried out 'death to Jews'. The condemnation of Dreyfus was a win for the army, the state and anti-Semitic groups, but there was a snag. Not long after the guilty verdict had been read, the French military learned of the actual culprit – Ferdinand Walsin Esterhazy.

Born into an illegitimate line of aristocracy, Esterhazy had failed his way up the ranks of the army, thanks to his connections. A gambling addict, he'd begun selling secrets to Schwartzkoppen after he'd run out of money. In 1896, the new head of French Intelligence, Lieutenant Colonel Georges Picquart, uncovered the mound of evidence linking Esterhazy to the crime; however, his efforts to investigate were blocked and he was hastily relieved of duty and reposted to Tunisia. That didn't mean that Picquart stopped calling for justice, and nor did Dreyfus's family, who made complaints about Esterhazy to the military. Word was starting to creep out and eventually in January 1898, in a bid to avoid total scandal, Esterhazy was put on trial. This was very much for show, as despite the evidence against him, it would have been too humiliating for the military for Esterhazy to be found guilty, and so on 11 January, he was acquitted. This was what sparked Émile Zola to publish *J'Accuse*, declaring: '*the truth is on the march, and nothing shall stop it.*'

What followed was a spurious series of events which divided not only those involved in the case but the nation at large into two separate factions. Those that supported Dreyfus decried this as an example of loss of individual rights, whereas those that saw Dreyfus as a traitor argued a more nationalistic angle – this was a fight for the very soul of France, a history and heritage to which Jews like Dreyfus did not belong. In February, Zola was arrested and found guilty of criminal libel, and similar trumped-up charges were aimed at Picquart, who was accused of forging the evidence that exposed Esterhazy. Anti-Semitic riots broke out across France, and as the months progressed new leaks kept springing up, with newspapers publishing more of the mounting evidence against Esterhazy. France's Minister for War, Godefroy Cavaignac, was drafted in to reinvestigate the case, and on 7 July 1898, he publicly presented final proof of Dreyfus's guilt, citing the original 1894 letters, as well as one from 1896 which showed attachés from Italy and Germany discussing Dreyfus's successful espionage. Picquart called for the letters to be re-examined as he knew them to be fakes and this was carried out in August. It turned out Picquart was right, as on holding the 1896 letter up to a lamp, it could be seen that it was actually multiple letters pasted together – a forgery.

THE ZOLA CONSPIRACY

In 1902, Émile Zola was found dead in his home of carbon monoxide poisoning. Immediately, conspiracy theories began – had he killed himself, unable to live with Dreyfus's guilty verdict? Had he been killed by Zionists? Then in 1953, reports emerged of a death-bed confession by an anti-Dreyfusard stove-fitting contractor who had been working on Zola's neighbour's house and taken the opportunity to stuff Zola's chimney and cause the carbon monoxide leak. It's still not known if this is true, but many have taken it as fact.

The culprit was found, one Lieutenant-Colonel Hubert-Joseph Henry, Picquart's former deputy. Henry was detained on 30 August and admitted his guilt; however, the next day, he was found dead in his cell – an apparent suicide. Anti-Semitic newspaper *La Libre Parole* began a campaign heralding Henry as a martyr who had only done his duty for France, and generated more than 25,000 donations towards '*the Henry Monument*'. Meanwhile, Esterhazy had fled to Britain, where in September he confessed his guilt to Rachel Beer, the editor of British newspaper the *Observer*. Alfred Dreyfus was innocent – though still not in the eyes of the law. France's government couldn't stall any longer and, despite pressure from nationalist groups, in June 1899, Dreyfus's 1894 military ruling was overturned. Still a prisoner, Dreyfus was returned to France for a second trial, and in a strange move seemingly desperate to still please nationalists, he was found guilty of treason but with '*extenuating circumstances*'. Dreyfus appealed this and was informed he would be pardoned, but only if he accepted his guilt. Exhausted and weak from his time at Devil's Island, Dreyfus just wanted to return home to his wife and children – he accepted the terms.

Finally, in 1906, Dreyfus was officially exonerated, and almost immediately he rejoined the French Army. Still, he remained a focal point for anti-Semitic hatred and was the target of an assassination attempt in 1908. Indeed, anti-Semitism would remain at a heightened state, and the remaining tendrils of its cultural boom were about to take a very nasty form.

Part V

THE TWENTIETH CENTURY

THE CONCENTRATION CAMP LIE

In 1901, Herbert Kitchener was under considerable pressure. He had just taken over as the British commander-in-chief in the Second Boer War and was trying to turn the tide against a rise in Boer guerrilla warfare. Yet somehow, the sudden change in tactics wasn't the greatest thorn in his side – that honour went to a middle-aged woman from Cornwall, Emily Hobhouse, or as Kitchener called her, '*That bloody woman!*'

Before Hobhouse's involvement, the Boer War was already a bit of a convoluted mess. In the mid-1800s, many people of Dutch descent had moved from the South African British area of the Cape Colony, to create their own independent republics, the Transvaal and the Orange Free State. The people of these new states became known as 'Boers' – the Dutch and Afrikaans word for farmers. However, the British weren't too keen on having these republics outside of their control and attempts to annex them into the British fold resulted in the First Boer War in 1880. The Boers won, but the British weren't giving up, especially as Boer lands were rich in diamonds and gold. In 1896, an attempt was made to overthrow Transvaal's government, which unsurprisingly led Transvaal to form an alliance with the Orange Free State. Embarrassed by its loss, and more than a little keen to cash in on the gold trade, Britain readied itself for war. Officially, the war would be to prevent the Boers from taking South Africa and to protect so-called 'Kaffirs' (black Africans) from Boer mistreatment. Realistically, though, when the Second Boer War broke out in October 1899, the real fight, at least for Britain, was for pride, power and money.

In September 1900, the last of the major Boer cities had fallen and Britain believed it had won. Job done, its commander-in-chief returned to England and handed the reins over to Kitchener, who would clean up any last scraps of fighting. Unfortunately, the British were very wrong. The war wasn't over, its tactics had just changed, with the Boers adapting to guerrilla warfare. To combat this, Kitchener opted for a scorched-earth approach, burning down homes, crops and supplies. This left many Boer women and children homeless and so refugee camps began to be built to house them. These camps soon expanded to take in Boers who had surrendered, and with this structure in place, it didn't take long for the British to think of another way to utilize their camp system.

In Kitchener's words, '*The women left in farms give complete intelligence to the Boers and all our movements and feed commandos in their neighbourhood*' – these women were just as much of a threat as the Boer soldiers and so it was decided that they, along with their children, should be rounded up and forced into camps. The use of concentration camps was nothing new, becoming prevalent during the Cuban War of Independence, and now the Boer War would be the third major war in recent years to use this tactic. In 1901, the camps moved beyond the Boers to include the black population who were being used by both sides as slaves, servants and conscripted military. By June 1901, the British had recorded that there were 85,410 inmates in its white camps and 32,350 in its black camps.

Earlier that year, in January, anti-war campaigner Emily Hobhouse managed to get permission to visit some of the concentration camps. The military barred her from viewing more than a handful of the white camps, but the little that she did manage to see would be enough. On returning to Britain in June 1901, Hobhouse published her findings in an explosive exposé, *Report of a Visit to the Camps of Women and Children in the Cape and Orange River Colonies*. According to Hobhouse, disease and malnutrition were rampant in the camps, and poor hygiene, combined with lack of adequate medical care, meant that mothers were unable to help their dying children – in short: '*To keep these camps going is murder to the children.*' Yet Hobhouse's bleak account was decidedly different from what the government was telling the British public. They'd promised that the camps were a voluntary safe harbour from the war, ensuring humanitarian aid to all refugees. This was a lie.

While Hobhouse had been compiling her report, Kitchener had ordered British Major George Goodwin to do the same. He'd found '*people are barefooted and in rags*', camps with little to no sanitation or shelter, endemic levels of diarrhoea and measles among child inmates and non-existent modern medical care to treat them. Each week, thousands more people were being taken to camps that already couldn't care for their existing captives, and the new inmates soon found themselves drowning in mud, disease and death. When Hobhouse wrote that she had witnessed '*a death rate such as had never been known except in the times of the Great Plagues. ... the whole talk was of death ... who died yesterday, who lay dying today, and who would be dead tomorrow ...*' this wasn't news to the British military, but rather an outside reflection of what Goodwin had reported. Yet very little was done to improve things, with the military instead opting to censor whatever they could and informing the government that civilian aid and support could not be deployed.

Yet, as it so often does, the truth finally came out in June 1901, with the publication of Hobhouse's exposé. The British public were shocked and Parliament was quick to demand answers. St John Brodrick, the Secretary of State for War, declared that there were 63,127 people in all the camps – if he knew he wasn't telling the truth, or simply hadn't been provided with the correct figure, is uncertain, but Brodrick was vastly downplaying the severity of the situation. By this point, there were closer to 117,760 people imprisoned. The opposition leader, Lloyd George, accused the British government and military of pursuing '*a policy of extermination against women and children. Not a direct policy of extermination, but a policy that would have that effect.*' Brodrick shrugged this off, replying that he'd heard it really wasn't *that* bad. Perhaps the best encapsulation of this form of government defence was that proffered by Winston Churchill to *The Times* newspaper on 28 June 1901: '*Would they* [the opposition] *have refused to accept responsibility for the Boer women and children left in the devastated districts? ... Have left the women sitting hungry amid the ruins? The mind revolts from such ideas: and so, we come to concentration camps, honestly believing they involve the minimum of suffering.*' Yes, the camps were bad, yes, people were dying, but it was the most humanitarian option available – there was apparently no middle ground to be found.

Amidst this malaise of inaccurate governmental data and illogical arguments, something crucial was lost – the tens of thousands of black people interned at the camps. Arguably, their conditions were far worse than those found in the Afrikaaner camps. Supplies to these camps were at a lower priority, with shipments of alcohol for British troops often put higher than food and medicine for the '*native camps*'. In March 1901, it was recorded that food at one camp was so scarce that prisoners had been forced to pick at the long-since rotted carcasses of nearby animals. Yet Emily Hobhouse hadn't seen these camps and so although she stated that their conditions were supposed to be terrible, the captives' plight remained invisible and, thus, uncared for. Instead, the press coverage of the concentration camps focused wholly on the visible white women and children. In a way, for the British government, this was a bit of a coup and they pushed forward with turning the camps into a '*women's issue*'. They played on the notion that women, like Hobhouse, didn't understand the brutality of war, which was why they found the camps so barbaric, yet, as it did in the home, a woman's touch could work wonders and so the government agreed to form a women's group to investigate how the camps might be improved.

Despite being the obvious choice, Emily Hobhouse was not permitted to join this group. She had proved herself far too outspoken. Instead, the government plumped for Millicent Fawcett, a leading campaigner for women's suffrage who had handily just written an article for the *Westminster Gazette* defending the camps as '*necessary*'. Under her leadership, in July 1901, the Fawcett Commission set out to investigate the camps – notably, despite urging from Hobhouse, the commission only deemed it essential to report on the white camps. The findings of

---

LIVES LOST

In the white camps, over 26,000 died, and of those, most were children. Unfortunately, in the black camps, the exact fatality rate is unknown, thanks to far less effort being made to record numbers of prisoners, though it's estimated that at least 20,000 lost their lives.

---

the Fawcett Commission mirrored those of Hobhouse, but with one clear difference. While Hobhouse had blamed the British military and government for the lack of supplies, medicine and shelter that resulted in high child fatality rates, Millicent Fawcett argued that the mothers were, at least in part, to blame. She stated that Boer women had no concept of modern medical care: '*A large number of deaths in the concentration camps have been directly or obviously caused by the noxious compounds given by Boer women to their children.*' That most of the imprisoned women had no access to better medicine than the folk cures they could scrape together was ignored, and when Fawcett's report was released in 1902, it was her placement of blame that much of the press picked up on. Britain used the confined mothers as a scapegoat, with Kitchener also blaming them: '*It is impossible to fight against the criminal neglect of the mothers, I do not like the idea of using force ... but I am considering whether some of the worst cases could not be tried for manslaughter.*'

Ultimately, the British government agreed to act on the advice of the Fawcett Commission and improve conditions in the camps. Yet, it was too little too late, as the Boer War would end in May 1902, meaning that the camps only began improvements for a few months before they were shut down altogether. The British government's refusal to admit to Emily Hobhouse's claims, the military's defiant attempts at censorship, and the multitude of lies spread between would result in tens of thousands of deaths.

THE PROTOCOLS OF ZION

In the years immediately after the Dreyfus Affair, a strange document surfaced in Russia, titled *The Protocols of the Elders of Zion*. This rambling, lengthy read described how for centuries Jewish people had been secretly manipulating global affairs and put forward a plan for their world domination. This document is a forgery, a Frankenstein compilation of the 1800s' anti-Semitic greatest hits, but just because something is fake doesn't mean it's not dangerous. It would not be an understatement to say that millions of people have died thanks to its contents. *Protocols* sparked pogroms, helped pave the way for the Holocaust, and remains a staple within white supremacy movements. But why was it written in the first place and what made such an obvious lie endure?

We still don't know the exact source of *Protocols*; however, there are multiple theories, and most historians agree that it was written between the height of the Dreyfus Affair in 1898 and the beginning of a wave of pogroms in Russia in 1903. The most likely explanation for its inception was that it was written by Russian conservatives and members of the secret police who were operating in France at the time of the Dreyfus Affair. Much of the text of the *Protocols* is lifted directly from anti-Dreyfus publications, as well as nine of its chapters being heavily plagiarized from French political satire *The Dialogue in Hell Between Machiavelli and Montesquieu*. In fact, in 1902, when the conservative Russian journalist Mikhail Osipovich Men'shikov broke the news of a 3,000-year-old '*secret conspiracy against humanity*', he traced its origin back to France. Alleging that a woman from St Petersburg who was now living in the country had been given the '*thick manuscript*' by a French journalist after it was stolen from a secret Jewish vault in Nice. The woman then translated the manuscript into Russian, with this translation becoming the first published edition of *Protocols* which appeared in Russia in 1903. The supposed original French manuscript has never appeared again, and there is no concrete evidence that offers a solid glimpse of the mysterious woman's identity.

Before *Protocols* was first published in Russia in 1903, the country had undergone a series of rapid changes in terms of its cultural understanding and treatment of Jewish people. On 13 March 1881, Tsar Alexander II was assassinated by an anti-tsarist group, the People's Will. Under Alexander II, an attempt had been made to move Jewish communities away from segregation and assimilate them into Russian society and culture. However, following his death, this would all be swiftly reversed. Rumours swirled that it was actually the Jews who had killed Alexander II. Pogroms broke out, and in 1882, Alexander III put in place a series of anti-Semitic laws, which restricted where Russia's Jews could live, what they could own, and their business practices. In the midst of all of this came a revival of blood libel conspiracies, which only furthered distrust and hatred towards Jewish communities. In response, there was a huge flood of emigration, as Russia's Jews left en masse to seek better lives. But for those who stayed, things would get even worse as the twentieth century dawned.

At Easter 1903, the city of Kishinev (now Chişinău in the Republic of Moldova) started a domino effect that would lead to an epidemic of pogroms across Russia. For the last few years, the city's most popular newspaper, *Bessarabetz*, under the editorship of Pavel Krushevan, had leaned heavily on rhetoric, running headlines such as '*Death to the Jews!*' and '*Crusade Against the hated race!*'. In 1902, Krushevan first attempted a blood libel story, but this nugget of fake news failed to rouse anyone. However, his 1903 effort would be more successful – the newspaper fabricated an elaborate murder plot, linking the February death of a young boy and the recent suicide of a girl in one of Kishinev's hospitals to the Jewish community, and stated that the children's blood would be used during Passover. Over the course of three days, forty-nine people were killed, hundreds injured and more than a thousand houses razed to the ground. The massacre at Kishinev caused an international outcry, yet very little was done about it. While Jewish groups in America arranged aid and assisted in emigration, Tsar

Nicholas II sat on his hands. The reason for this was partly due to the Russian government's overriding opinion of '*The Jewish Question*' – in the minds of Nicholas II and his ilk, Russian Jews weren't real Russians, they were aliens who had to have oppressive sanctions thrust upon them. Should they protect them from pogroms and violence, it would only result in a backlash from the booming right-wing nationalistic movement – it just wasn't worth the bother.

This lack of clear action or sanctions would only get worse. In the summer of 1903, Pavel Krushevan used another of his newspapers, *Znamya*, to release the first published edition of *The Protocols of the Elders of Zion*, with serialized segments appearing throughout August and September. From there, publications of *Protocols* within Russia snowballed, particularly in 1905 and 1906. In January 1905, the First Russian Revolution broke out, and this rise in tensions resulted in yet another spate of pogroms. Again, Nicholas II didn't act. This time though, it was because the pogroms were a great distraction, as if people were enacting violence towards Russia's Jews, then they weren't focusing their energy on him. It was less a case of state-sanctioned anti-Semitism, and more of state-allowed, which was why of the estimated 650 pogroms that took place between 1903 and 1906, many saw the active participation of local authorities and police.

By the 1920s, *The Protocols of the Elders of Zion* had gone global, with translations of it appearing in books and newspapers across the world. Following the 1903–6 pogroms, more Jewish people had emigrated from Russia and Eastern Europe, and this tide of migration hadn't really let up, with many countries continuing to grapple with their new influx of people. This was combined with the fallout of the First World War and *Protocols* soon became most embraced by those countries that not only had a newly enlarged Jewish populace but had also been emotionally and financially devastated by the war. The most prominent of these was Germany. *Protocols* helped explain why they'd lost the war, the crushing economic blows of the Treaty of Versailles, and the chaos of the 1918–19 German revolution. They weren't to blame; it was all a Jewish conspiracy. It was no coincidence that *Protocols* began flooding the market in 1919, the year Germans were at their most emotionally vulnerable, desperate for a scapegoat.

A DISASTROUS TREATY

Signed on 28 June 1919, the Treaty of Versailles was one of several treaties that ended the First World War. However, it is notable for a clause that essentially had Germany take almost sole responsibility for the war, resulting in loss of land, resources and military power, and crucially – hefty payments, which decimated the German economy. By 1923, hyperinflation had so badly eroded the country's finances that money was useless and children could be seen playing with it in the street.

That's not to say it wasn't a known fact at this time that *Protocols* was a forgery. In August 1921, British newspaper *The Times* published conclusive evidence that showed the *Protocols* to be a lie. But these were rare voices in a sea of conspiracy theories. Historian Dr Wolfram Meyer zu Uptrup estimates that, from 1920 onwards, following the formation of the National Socialist German Workers' Party (later known as the Nazi Party), 70 per cent of articles on Jews in the party's official newspaper, *Völkischer Beobachter*, contained elements from *Protocols*. Indeed, the *Protocols* would be a major feature of Nazi ideology and policy, going on to infiltrate everything from schooling to press and legislation.

THE PROPAGANDA WAR

From the end of July through August 1914, many countries joined what would become known as the First World War at an unprecedented rate. On 28 June 1914, the heir to the throne of the Austro-Hungarian Empire, Archduke Franz Ferdinand, was assassinated by a Serbian nationalist. By 28 July Austria–Hungary had declared war on Serbia, with Germany soon backing them. Within the next month, battle lines had been drawn, with France, Russia and Great Britain forming an allied opposing force. With five of the greatest European powers involved, this war wouldn't be confined to Europe, and in the coming months and years each side would fight to bring the likes of America and China into the fray. Yet in August 1914, the immediate focus was at home. For any country to come out on top, it needed its own people to not just support the war, but be willing to join it and, if needed, make the ultimate sacrifice. Across Europe, propaganda machines leapt into motion.

It did not begin well. Take, for example, Britain, which by the end of the war would have arguably the greatest if not the most ruthless propaganda machine of any country involved, but at the start fumbled things spectacularly. Britain had joined the war partly because of the Treaty of London, which had long granted Belgium its neutrality and called upon Europe's 'Great Powers' to defend this. When Germany invaded Belgium on 4 August, it had broken its part of the treaty and essentially violated European treaty and international law. For Britain, it was assumed that this reasoning would be enough to bring the nation behind the war cause. A treaty was no mere scrap of paper; it was a symbol of international law and a peacefully functioning continent, surely something every British man would agree was worth fighting and perhaps dying for. Unfortunately, it was quickly discovered that this wasn't the case, and such vague international political semantics was not enough to rouse a nation and rally the troops.

To get the public on board, it was clear another tactic was needed, a more emotive one. The German invasion of Belgium had been bloody, and by 8 August, nearly 850 civilians were dead, many of whom had been executed in the street. Then, towards the end of August, German troops began to set ablaze and pillage villages and towns. This kind of bloodshed was exactly the human interest angle the British propaganda machine was after, but to spin the razing of homes, eviction of families, and killing of civilians would be a risky move – after all, not twenty years before, Britain had essentially done the same thing during the Boer War, under the command of Lord Kitchener, who was now Britain's Secretary of State for War. A new focus was seized on – sexual violence, with the invasion of Belgium rebranded as the Rape of Belgium.

This wasn't without some precedence, as during the invasion there were reports of Belgian women and girls enduring rape and mutilation; however, it should be noted that these horrific cases were an isolated minority. But not according to Britain, which spun a story of systemic abuse that seemingly all German soldiers were participating in. By the end of 1914, British writer William Le Queux was describing the German military as: *'one vast gang of Jack the Rippers'* who were all partaking in *'wild orgies of blood and debauchery* ... [and] *the ruthless violation and killing of defenceless women, girls, and children of tender age'*. This notion of widespread sexual violence became emblematic across the Allied nations, gradually becoming stylized into cartoons and propaganda posters. It wasn't unusual for a push for war bonds or military recruitment to be headed with a lurid illustration of a woman under attack. The legitimate suffering of women in Belgium and France had been transformed into something else entirely, and it was becoming harder to tell those stories of true atrocities from those that had been fabricated for the war effort.

Germany understandably was not pleased with how it was being internationally labelled and in October 1914 it gathered its greatest cultural and intellectual figures to release a manifesto debunking '*the lies*' being spread by the Allies. *The Manifesto of the Ninety-Three* claimed that no unlawful violence had been committed against Belgian citizens, though it noted that, *had* there been violence, it would have been the civilians' fault. Although this gained public support within Germany, it didn't take off elsewhere. In 1915, the Germans tried again, this time releasing the *White Book*, a purported report of the atrocities committed against their citizens and military, which included claims that Belgian civilians had carried out sadistic acts against German soldiers, including everything from eye gouging to castration. Most of the *White Book* was a fabrication, falsely elaborating on events, omitting testimony that contradicted them, and heavily editing information. But again, this didn't mean it didn't take off within Germany, where newspapers reported on a young boy coming across a bucket of German soldiers' eyes, a French priest who wore a necklace of dead men's rings, and Belgians swapping German cigars for explosives.

By 1915, a new propaganda game had begun – wooing neutral countries. Though the Netherlands had made it clear it intended to remain neutral, there were two other big prizes up for grabs – America and China. Once more, an arms race of words began with Britain the titan of Allied propaganda and Germany the major representative of the Central Powers. The first port of call was America. On 7 May 1915, the British ocean liner the RMS *Lusitania* was sunk by a German U-boat, killing over a thousand passengers and crew, including 123

Americans. Germany justified the attack as the ship had been carrying munitions, but Britain claimed this was another example of German atrocities and their '*barbarism*'. Not long after the sinking, German artist Karl Goetz made a satirical medal that mocked Britain's irresponsibility in using a passenger vessel to carry munitions. However, Goetz accidentally put the wrong date on the medal – 5 May 1915. Britain seized upon this, falsely alleging that this was proof Germany had always planned to attack American citizens and created these medals to reward the perpetrators.

One victory under Britain's belt, and another propaganda coup was about to land in their lap, in the form of British nurse Edith Cavell, who in August that year had been captured by the Germans after helping Allied prisoners escape occupied Belgium. The British propaganda machine leaned heavily on America, creating a US campaign to free the '*innocent*' woman from Germany's '*barbaric*' clutches. Ultimately, Cavell was executed in October and the British government spent approximately £120,000 in creating propaganda around her death. A false story emerged that at her execution, Cavell had fainted and a German officer had shot the unconscious woman. On 23 October 1915, the *New York World* declared Cavell's death '*worse than a crime!*', and in the following weeks, she became seen as a martyr. Germany tried to defend itself, but with tensions already high from the *Lusitania* disaster, it was a losing battle, and gone was their chance of wooing America or convincing them to remain neutral.

Still, China looked like it might be a good prospect. From

the outbreak of war, Germany, as well as France and Britain, had made concerted efforts to infiltrate the country with propaganda, and despite efforts by Britain to cut Germany off from its colonies, such as Hong Kong, Germany had maintained its presence. Indeed, after the war, it was reported that up until 1917, many Chinese people assumed Germany would ultimately win. This changed when Germany declared it would be using unrestricted submarine warfare. On 17 February 1917, a German submarine destroyed the French ship SS *Athos*, killing over 500 Chinese workers. Unsurprisingly, come March, the Chinese were rapidly turning against Germany, with another blow coming in April, when America began assisting the Allies in flooding China with propaganda.

BEHIND THE MACHINE

Canadian novelist and politician Sir Gilbert Parker was tasked with running British propaganda to America, with Count Johann von Bemstorff manning things on the German end. Though both initially got off to a good start, Bemstorff was denied money to fund propaganda journalism in the US, allowing Parker to capture the market by mid-1915. To make matters worse, a briefcase full of German propaganda plans was stolen on the New York Subway and leaked to the press, obliterating any chance of Germany winning the country's favour.

This brought an incredibly gruesome hoax. Back in February 1917, it had been reported by the *North China Daily News* that the Germans had created a '*corpse factory*' or '*Kadaververwertungsanstalt*', in which the bodies of its soldiers were melted down to make glycerine. Come April, this one-off story was revived with even gorier details. British newspapers *The Times* and *Daily Mail* now proffered supposedly first-hand accounts of how the factory turned German soldiers into '*oils, fats and pig food*'. In actuality, the original story came from a German newspaper which described how the bodies of animals were being used for this purpose. The British propaganda office had merely replaced the German word '*Kadaver*' with the similar sounding word for human remains, '*Cadaver*'. This simple switch created an international frenzy, and though Germany was quick to point out the lie, it was too little too late. Chinese officials were horrified by what they'd heard and by August, China had declared war and officially joined the Allies.

Following the end of the First World War, the delight with which British propagandists vied at dinner parties to take credit for the corpse factory hoax shows both how much propaganda meant to the war and how easy it had been to lie. For the victors, there were no immediate consequences, while the losers bore the brunt. The war had popularized something called atrocity propaganda, a technique that had existed throughout history, but had never before been so utilized by so many nations. If you can demonize your enemy, and prove – falsely or otherwise – that they are capable of the unthinkable, then you can transform them into a monstrous other that must be defeated.

It's an ingenious way of gaining support and marshalling action – a kind of psychological warfare that is often only discovered once it has completed its job. The First World War had finessed atrocity propaganda, proved its worth, and since then, it has become a key part of international politics and warfare.

THE SPANISH FLU CENSORS

On 28 September 1918, 200,000 people gathered in downtown Philadelphia to celebrate the impending armistice of the First World War and raise funds for American war bonds. As a parade marched through the streets and crowds cheered, something horrific was taking root. Within seventy-two hours of the celebration, Philadelphia's hospitals were full to capacity. The Spanish flu had hit, and six weeks after the parade floats were cleared, an estimated 12,000 people were dead, and the city's funeral homes were unable to cope with the influx of bodies. It's now common knowledge that there really is no good time for a global pandemic to happen, but arguably the so-called Spanish flu could not have come at a worse time.

In early 1918, several incidences of what we now know to be a strain of the influenza virus were found in America, Europe and Asia. The most notable of these cases was that of Albert Gitchel, a cook at a military camp in Kansas. His diagnosis of the then mystery flu, on 4 March 1918, kicked off its first wave.

It was the last year of the First World War, and soldiers were travelling back and forth across countries in often cramped and squalid conditions. This was the case for the soldiers at Gitchel's camp – those that survived the outbreak were shipped back to the front, several likely still unknowingly infected. Soon troops from Britain, France, Italy and Spain were falling ill, and by early summer cases were registered in China, Australia, North Africa and India. This was followed by a disastrous second wave in August. Central America, South America, West Africa and South Africa joined the spread, and by September, almost all of Europe was buckling under the rate of infections. What made the virus so much worse was that it tended to kill the young, with those under five, between twenty-five and forty, and over sixty-five most susceptible – soldiers would survive the worst of the war, only to die from the flu. In all, it's estimated that roughly one-third of the world's population was infected with the virus, with at least 50 million people dying, mostly during the flu's second wave – a number that arguably was avoidable.

As we've already seen, at the time of the Spanish flu's rise, many countries that were engaged in the First World War were actively censoring their press. An epidemic was sure to lower public morale, something no government wanted, and so most of those nations in the midst of the war added reporting of the flu into their censorship boundaries. This stance was best described by a Public Health Commissioner for Chicago, who said that it was paramount in wartime to do '*nothing to interfere with the morale of the community ... it is our duty to keep the people from fear. Worry kills more people than the epidemic.*' The logic behind that statement is flimsy at best; however, some rationalization can be given to the initial censorship action, in that during the pandemic's first wave, many medical professionals assumed it to be a particularly nasty strain of flu, not the deadly phenomenon it would become. Still, that justification quickly ran out by May–June 1918, just before the second wave hit. At that point, the spread was rapidly growing, as were fatality rates – to not inform the public and to deny the public health threat at play was actively choosing to put millions of lives in danger.

One country that stands out in all this is Spain. Remaining neutral throughout the war, it had no reason to censor news of the increasing global epidemic. From May 1918 onwards, the flu blanketed the country's newspapers, especially after Spain's king, Alfonso XIII, fell ill with it. As one of the very few nations publicly talking about the pandemic, Spain became unequivocally linked to it. In late May 1918, the first the British public knew of the virus was from reports in the *Daily Mail* and *Daily Express*, which frantically spoke about a '*mysterious epidemic*' ravaging

Spain. In response, the *British Medical Journal* called out the reports as '*alarmist*'. The *Daily Mail* was quick to clean up its mistake: in a June article entitled '*Is Influenza Coming?*' medical experts reminded readers that the flu was just a bad cold and advised that the best way to prevent it was to '*maintain a cheery outlook on life*', as those who were in '*depressed states*' were more likely to catch flu. This became something of a universal stance – only Spain had the bad flu, and any cases in other countries were just ordinary everyday flu. As late as 22 August 1918, Italy's interior minister was still desperately denying claims of a deadly flu outbreak, while Philadelphia's super spreader September parade went ahead despite warnings from doctors, as city officials didn't want to cause any public concern.

This omission and misinformation led to conspiracy theories, with one June 1918 article in *The Times* causing international

WHAT'S IN A NAME?

The name of the Spanish flu comes from Spain being so vocal about the pandemic. This led many to believe it had originated in Spain, with other popular names for the virus including the Spanish Lady. Interestingly, in Spain, the outbreak was often referred to as the French flu. We still don't know exactly where the virus originated, but many historians cite America as the most likely source.

fear after the writer pondered if the virus might actually be German germ warfare. In other spheres, everything from jazz music to contamination of soil was blamed, and even a punishment from God bestowed on those who sang '*lewd songs*' was pointed to as the cause. Still, by the end of summer 1918, it was clear that there was a health crisis, and even if people didn't know exactly what it was, they wanted some kind of protection. In the place of clear governmental guidance, brands stepped in. German lozenge brand Formamint claimed its products, made from formaldehyde, milk and pepsin-hydrochloric acid, prevented the Spanish flu. Meanwhile, bone marrow and egg mix Chymol touted that its foodstuff prevented death, and Australian adverts for Aspirin brand Aspro advocated taking dangerous amounts to fight flu.

Fortunately, by the autumn of 1918, the censorship veil had started to drop – between major disasters such as the parade in Philadelphia and rising death rates, public health mandates were swiftly enforced. Mask wearing, hand washing, and forms of social distancing were encouraged. Ironically, as mask mandates were enforced in multiple American cities and states, governmental advertising turned to shaming those who weren't doing everything possible to protect public health, coming up with the term '*mask slackers*' and the slogan '*Coughs and Sneezes Spread Diseases: As Dangerous as Poison Gas Shells.*' We'll never know exactly how many lives could have been saved if countries hadn't enforced pandemic censorship, but their denials did have a major impact on public health and the ability people had to protect themselves.

ANNA OR ANASTASIA?

. . . .

On 27 February 1920, a young woman was fished out of the waters of Berlin's Landwehr Canal. She had no purse, no papers, and seemingly no memory of who she was, authorities admitting her to a mental hospital in Dalldorf Asylum under the name '*Madame Unknown*'. Under examination, two things were discovered: the first was extensive scarring all over her body, and the second was that she could speak Russian. For over a year this was all that was known about Madame Unknown. Then, sometime in the autumn of 1921, the mysterious woman called over a nurse and pointed to a magazine picture of the Russian royal family. Something had jogged her memory, or perhaps she just decided now was the time to break her silence – her name, she said, was Grand Duchess Anastasia Romanov.

Three years earlier, in 1917, as the rest of the world's focus was on the still-raging First World War, the status quo of Russia had been upturned. Since the First Russian Revolution in 1905, tensions within the country had remained high and Russia's involvement in the world war hadn't helped things. Tsar Nicholas II hadn't been prepared to go to war, let alone one of this magnitude, and the Russian people paid for his lack of clear economic or military planning. Conscription policies left farmlands undermanned, which resulted in very little food. Factory workers were made to work so many hours that strikes and riots broke out. Meanwhile, the Russian military was ill-equipped to fight and prone to mutiny. Nicholas II left to command his troops, leaving his wife, Tsarina Alexandra, in charge at home, and she deliberately surrounded herself with ministers that were weaker than her husband, exasperating an already tenuous situation. The Russian people began to turn once more to revolutionaries, with Bolshevik support surging. In March 1917, during the nominally named February Revolution, Nicholas II abdicated the throne, and over the next year, the Bolsheviks began to seize power. Nicholas, Alexandra and their children, Olga, Tatiana, Maria, Anastasia and Alexei were imprisoned under house arrest until it was decided that for the Bolsheviks to retain control, no member of the Romanov royal family could be left to reclaim the throne.

In the early hours of 17 July 1918, the family and their closest servants were gathered in the basement of a house in Ekaterinburg (now known as Yekaterinburg) and executed. Their bodies were spirited away, secretly buried in Koptyaki forest. At first, only Nicholas's death was announced, but it didn't take much imagination to realize that, with the rest of the family missing, they too had probably died. For many, this was a hard pill to swallow, but the name that kept coming back up was that of seventeen-year-old Anastasia. Of all the Romanov children, she'd been the odd one out, full of life, cheeky and a born wit – surely, somehow, Anastasia had managed to survive. According to Madame Unknown, she had. The young woman claimed that she (Anastasia Romanov) hadn't died during the execution, but merely been knocked unconscious. A Polish soldier, Alexander Tchaikovsky, secretly carried her to safety and, along with his family, Anastasia had fled to Bucharest. There she fell pregnant by Alexander, who was soon killed in a knife fight. Anastasia gave the baby away for adoption, before travelling to Berlin in the hope of getting help from her godmother, Princess Irene of Prussia. However, on arriving in Berlin, she became overwhelmed by despair and attempted suicide – jumping into the Landwehr Canal.

THE OTHER ROMANOVS

Anna Tchaikovsky was not the first nor the last person to claim to be a surviving Romanov child. Multiple imposters for Anastasia and each of her siblings have appeared over the years, including former CIA agent Michael Goleniewski, who claimed to be Alexei; Marga Boodts, whose insistence that she was Olga allegedly resulted in financial backing from Pope Pius XII; and another Anastasia pretender, Eugenia Smith, who even landed a book deal.

Word of this tale soon spread and, in 1922, Princess Irene actually visited the Dalldorf Asylum to see if the story was true. On meeting 'Anastasia', Irene quickly proclaimed her as an imposter, but not every member of the Romanovs' extended family and friends did the same. By May 1922, 'Anastasia', now going as Anna Tchaikovsky, had gained enough support to be freed from the asylum and moved into the home of

Baron Arthur von Kleist. The reason for such belief in her story wasn't just desperation though. After announcing the death of Nicholas II in 1918, the new Soviet government appeared to keep changing their mind on whether they should declare the whole family dead. In 1919, they did, but said Left-Wing Revolutionaries had been responsible. In the coming years, this was changed – the women had survived but Nicholas and Alexei were dead; then in 1922, it was declared that the whole family was actually alive. This ever-changing story led to a great deal of conspiracy theory and rumour, to the point that Tchaikovsky's claims suddenly didn't seem that far-fetched.

Still, there were doubters: in 1927, a Berlin newspaper hired private detective Martin Knopf to uncover Tchaikovsky's true identity. After much digging, Knopf declared that Anna Tchaikovsky was, in fact, Polish factory worker Franziska Schanzkowska, who had been missing since early 1920. Her family was worried about her, as several years earlier, in 1916, Schanzkowska had been injured in a factory explosion, which left her with scarring over her body and frequent episodes of severe mental illness. Multiple people who knew Schanzkowska backed Knopf's findings, including her sister and brother. Still, Tchaikovsky remained steadfast, insisting she was Anastasia Romanov. In the following decades, Schanzkowska's family would retract their claims, not because they didn't believe Tchaikovsky was their sister, but because with the frenzy of Anastasia Romanov believers surrounding her, pressing for the truth seemed to be doing more harm than good, with Tchaikovsky's mental health worsening.

The Schanzkowska family out of the picture, Tchaikovsky was now encircled almost solely by people who believed her story and urged her to press for her royal dues, Tchaikovsky going on to launch a decades-long legal battle to claim the Romanov fortune. The case was lost in 1970, but Tchaikovsky, now living as Anna Anderson Manahan, would maintain her identity as Anastasia Romanov until her death in 1984.

In 1991, an excavation began in Yekaterinburg, which would unearth the remains of Nicholas II, his wife, Alexandra, and three of their daughters, likely Olga, Tatiana and Anastasia. The remains of the other two children, likely Maria and Alexei, were found nearby in 2007. Using a DNA sample from Britain's Prince Philip, it was conclusively determined that the remains were those of the Russian royal family. Anna Anderson Manahan was definitively not Anastasia Romanov. But who was she? In 1995, another test was done, this time using DNA from Franziska Schanzkowska's great-nephew. Finally, an answer came, the DNA match proved a maternal relation – Anna was indeed Franziska Schanzkowska.

Walter Duranty and the Great Famine

'*Liars go to hell*.' – In 1935, *New York Times* reporter and Pulitzer Prize winner Walter Duranty recalled how, when growing up, his evangelical grandmother would burn him whenever he lied –

'*liars go to hell and in hell it burns like this forever.*' For Walter, this explained not only why he'd not been too fond of his grandmother, but also his absolute aversion to lying, a way of life that for a journalist was a credit. Except Walter Duranty did lie; in fact, he was behind one of the greatest lies of the twentieth century, a lie that would ultimately help lead to the deaths of millions.

Born in Liverpool, England, in 1884, Duranty had reported on Russian affairs since the early days of the 1917 Russian Revolution. Interestingly, when *The New York Times* hired him as a Russian reporter in 1919, Duranty spoke no Russian and knew very little of the country, yet he threw himself into the role wholeheartedly. Despite his lack of knowledge and the fact that he was getting most of his information from press releases, Duranty initially tried to place himself as an expert on communism and Russia, proffering up incredibly anti-Soviet pieces that took fiery aim at the '*Bolshevist gang in Moscow*', and predicted that the regime and entire country would soon fall apart. Yet behind his bolshy swagger, much of his reporting, especially that of the Polish–Soviet War, contained vast amounts of misreporting and factual inaccuracies. Still, Duranty kept his job and in July 1921, he was selected as one of a handful of journalists to enter Russia to report on the country's famine. This was a career coup and tellingly Duranty wrote of the disaster that claimed millions of lives: '*Luck broke my way in the shape of the Russian Famine!*' The Russian Famine would indeed be the making of Duranty. He learned to speak Russian and navigate through Russia's strict censorship of the international press. By the mid-1920s, he had cemented himself a place as one of the West's leading Russian correspondents – his anti-Soviet tirades disappeared and, in return, he was showered with money, a large flat, a mistress, and not one but two coveted interviews with Joseph Stalin.

Nineteen twenty-eight was a big year for Stalin, who unveiled his first Five-Year Plan for Russia, which would collectivize agriculture and increase industrial output. However, the way Stalin intended to do this would come at a great human cost. Hordes of untrained peasants were moved to work in new factories, where they lived in squalid conditions and were in constant danger from the heavy machinery they had no experience in operating. Worse still was the impact of collectivizing agriculture. Privately owned farms were to be turned over to the government, and understandably many of those who lived on or owned these lands resisted the change, even going so far as to destroy their own crops and fields to prevent the government from taking them. Those that resisted were labelled '*Kulaks*' and deemed enemies of Russia. Stalin enlisted the help of everything from the army to the secret police in forcing peasants to hand over their land and, as for the Kulaks, it was decided they were to be: '*liquidated as a class*'. In 1930, Duranty came across a trainload of Kulaks being transported to exile in Central Asia, and he later described them as '*more like caged animals than human … debris and jetsam of the march to Progress*'. Yet, in his dispatches to *The New York Times*, Duranty spoke very little of the treatment of the Kulaks, focusing instead on the positive aspects of the Five-Year Plan, lauding Stalin as a leader whose achievements would '*show in history*' and who was restoring '*self-respect to a nation of liberated slaves*'.

In actuality, Stalin had essentially tied the peasantry to the land in a way they hadn't been since the emancipation of the serfs in 1861. Now, they were forced to send almost all their crops and food to the government, leaving them with next to nothing. In June 1932, Canadian agricultural expert Andrew Cairns reported to the British Foreign Office that while travelling in Russia he'd seen widespread famine: '*men, women, children, horses, and other workers are left to die in order that the Five Year Plan shall at least succeed on paper,*' with Ukraine, the Caucasus, Crimea, and Volga the hardest hit. Yet, according to Russia, there were no famines. In November 1932, the British Embassy met with Duranty and were surprised to learn that, despite never mentioning the famine in his articles, he was well aware one was currently raging, at one point noting: '*there are millions of people in Russia who it is safe to keep in want.*'

A PULITZER-WINNING LIE

In 1932, Duranty was awarded the Pulitzer Prize for his work in covering the implementation of Stalin's Five-Year Plan. *The New York Times* has since apologized for printing Walter Duranty's work during this time; however, despite numerous calls to have his Pulitzer Prize revoked, the Pulitzer board has refused, even stating in 2003 that it found '*no clear and convincing evidence of deliberate deception*'.

In December 1932, the Russian government enforced a new passport system that would allow more transportation of Kulaks and prevent the starving peasantry from moving to towns and cities. Then, in spring 1933, it barred those working on collective farmland from leaving – essentially entrapping those in famine areas and sentencing them to death from starvation. Duranty reported this as good news, once more omitting any mention of famine and applauding the Russian move to *'purge the city of undesirables'*. Part of the reason for Duranty's refusal to report on the famine was that he was working towards America officially recognizing the Soviet Union, which as one dispatch from the Moscow Chancery put it, he felt would have been *'an official tribute to his estimates of the Soviet condition ... leading possibly to his appointment on the arrival of an American Embassy in Moscow to some such post as that of the press attaché'*. It wasn't in Walter Duranty's interest for anyone outside Russia to know of the famine, so he did his best to silence it, not just in his own reporting, but in that of others.

Between 25 and 30 March 1933, Malcolm Muggeridge, a journalist for English newspaper the *Manchester Guardian*, finally broke the news of the famine in Ukraine. In a series of articles, he reported that not only were entire towns and villages starving to death but that this was overseen by *'well fed'* Russian troops, with residents resorting to cannibalism and suicide. The *Manchester Guardian* followed this on 30 March with an on-the-ground report by journalist Gareth Jones, which backed Muggeridge's claims. Yet a day later, Duranty used his far bigger platform in *The New York Times* to debunk the *Guardian's* findings, explaining that there were some incidences of people dying from malnutrition-related diseases, but that there was no famine, just less food than normal as Stalin's collectivization scheme settled in, concluding: *'To put it brutally, you can't make an omelette without breaking eggs.'* In the light of the words of the West's leading Russian correspondent, Muggeridge was vilified as a liar. But Gareth Jones hit back, writing a detailed account of the famine and its causes in the *Financial News*, but again Duranty claimed Jones to be exaggerating the situation. On 13 May, Jones took it to Duranty's home ground, writing a letter in *The New York Times* that stated Duranty was deliberately concealing the truth of the famine. Not long afterwards, the Soviet Union banned Jones from entering the country.

The famine in Ukraine (known there as the Holodomor) was at its worst, with people dying at a rate of up to 25,000 a day, but still, Duranty stuck to his guns – there was no famine. However, as the summer of 1933 began, more reports of starving Ukrainians started to spring up. Realizing that the truth would come out no matter what, Duranty desperately began to build a narrative that he'd always been reporting on the famine, linking it to his articles on the 1921 famine and bemoaning Russian censorship. However, this tactic wasn't proving fruitful, and after an American journalist, Frederick T. Birchall, reported that an estimated 4 million people had died from the famine, Duranty took it upon himself to visit the hardest-hit areas. On arriving in September 1933, Duranty sent back dispatches that proclaimed: *'Abundance found in North Caucasus'*, confirming that any famine was an *'absurdity'* and suggesting that the figures of millions of deaths had likely been a German conspiracy concocted by the Nazis. Yet on returning to Moscow, Duranty told the British Embassy quite a different story. There hadn't been '*abundance*' in the Caucasus; rather, between there and Volga, he estimated that at least 3 million must have died or been deported. Of Ukraine, he said it had '*been bled white*' and, together with the other regions, he believed 10 million had died as a result of collectivized agriculture.

Yet Duranty remained silent and, instead, intent on America recognizing the Soviet Union, he travelled to Washington, D.C., where he raved about Russia's achievements. On 16 November 1933, America officially recognized the Soviet Union, and at the celebratory dinner, Walter Duranty was cheered as the architect of this great achievement. On Christmas Day 1933, during an interview with Stalin, the dictator warmly congratulated Duranty: '*I might say that you bet on our horse to win when others thought it had no chance – and I am sure you have not lost by it.*' He hadn't. Walter Duranty was not punished for covering up the deaths of millions of people, he was rewarded for it. Of the victims of the famine, the exact death rate remains unclear, with estimates ranging between 5 and 10 million. Duranty's bold-faced lies and omissions contributed to this massive loss of life. Though several governments knew of the atrocities taking place, Duranty's failure to tell the truth prevented the public from forcing their countries to intervene and muddied the already murky communications between international bodies in regard to the Soviet Union.

The Tuskegee Experiment

· ·

First recorded in 1494, the sexually transmitted disease of syphilis has had somewhat of a globe-trotting venereal career, attaching itself to invading armies and international traders to further its spread. So, it's perhaps unsurprising that following the huge global deployment of armed forces during the First World War, by the 1930s, America had found itself in the midst of a syphilis epidemic, with an estimated one in ten Americans carriers. In what should have been a fortunate move, scientific research into syphilis was on the rise; however, not all of this research was good. In fact, one area would lead to one of the most horrific abuses of medical authority in history.

In the nineteenth century, following the Emancipation Proclamation and subsequent hysteria around miscegenation, American research into syphilis began to focus on the study of the racial division of the disease. What doctors came up with was a mutant Darwin-esque theory, that black people were inherently psychologically and morally inferior, resulting in higher cases of advanced syphilis. It should be noted that much of this research was done in impoverished areas, where people couldn't receive adequate treatment for the disease. Still, this became a fixed narrative – America's black population were prime carriers. As the twentieth century dawned, a new addition was made to the race theory – the neurosyphilis paradox. This claimed that although black people were more likely to get syphilis, they rarely contracted neurosyphilis. As explained in 1911 by Dr E. M. Hummell, a black person's brain was full of '*child-like euphoria of a care-free life*' and so was not evolved enough to contract neurosyphilis, which was the '*lot of the highly civilized white man*'. Again, this research was based less on any actual study and more on racist dogma, but the idea of racial nervous susceptibility to neurosyphilis took off. If incidences of neurosyphilis in black patients were allowed to fester, they could be studied and perhaps hold the key to better treatment or even a cure. But surely no patient would ever agree to a death sentence in the name of bad science – another route had to be found and an institute in Alabama seemed to be the perfect waypoint.

The Tuskegee Institute was founded in 1881, as part of an effort to expand education for the black community. In 1929, a group of mainly black physicians at the Institute had undertaken a study of syphilis, which included black patients; however, the data that they presented was unique in that it didn't show any racial hierarchical structure. This of course was totally overlooked, but the study itself brought the attention of the US Public Health Service (USPHS). They were looking for a place to launch a neurosyphilis paradox study and Tuskegee had experience in researching the disease as well as a large local black population who were currently experiencing a rise in syphilis cases – it was ideal.

In 1932, the USPHS started work on the Tuskegee Experiment. Many in the local community who had syphilis were untreated, mostly due to poor access to care and the high cost of treatment. This allowed the USPHS to deem the experiment a '*study in nature*' – the men they hoped to study currently weren't getting medical care, and so if they didn't treat them, was it *really* a violation of ethics? Yet the men signing up for the study weren't told that they wouldn't be treated. To secure a large pool for research, the government promised the community free examination and treatment for those experiencing '*bad blood*' whose symptoms could be due to anything from anaemia to syphilis itself. The examinations allowed the team to select men who had syphilis and then – under the promise of more treatment – use a spinal tap to test if the patient had early signs of neurosyphilis. By the end of the experiment's initial phase, the Tuskegee Experiment had 399 men with syphilis and a control group of 201 uninfected men.

However, in 1933, the experiment hit two mammoth hurdles. The first was that neurosyphilis takes years to develop, and none of the men was anywhere near the advanced stages that the USPHS hoped to study. They wanted to research the absolute last part of the disease's effect on the brain and then autopsy the body. As one of the leaders of the programme, Dr Oliver C. Wenger, put it: '*We have no further interest in these patients until they die.*' That wouldn't be happening for years, yet the experiment had only allotted itself enough money to run for six months. But the USPHS were impressed with the progress so far and so governmental funding was granted to continue the experiment indefinitely. With that issue solved, attention turned to the second problem – the participants. The men now needed to be tied into the experiment for their entire lives and made to believe that they were being cured of syphilis even as they actually died from it. Not only that, but each participant had to willingly sign their body away for autopsy. On the programme management's part, they only really cared about getting the body – not about the potentially decades' worth of lying they'd need to do to get there. This was flippantly discussed in a series of letters between Wenger and the experiment's on-site director, Raymond A. Vonderlehr. Wenger wrote: '*There is one danger in the latter plan and that is if the coloured population become aware that accepting free hospital care means a post-mortem, every darkey will leave Macon County,*' to which Vonderlehr responded: '*Naturally ... it is not my intention to let it be generally known that the main object of the present activities is the bringing of the men to necropsy.*'

The solution was to build community trust. Beyond the supposed medical care that the men were receiving, the experiment also provided free hot meals and transportation to the hospital as well as regular visits by friendly nurses. A conceit was created that this experiment would help change the community forever, saving lives and providing a new healthy future. On the back of this drumming up of support, patients were told that if they were to die under the programme, then their funeral costs would be covered – provided they signed over autopsy rights. The men went along with this, as they trusted the doctors looking after them and believed that this was just a sensible precaution – of course they wouldn't die, they were being made better.

By the mid-1940s, penicillin was widely available and had become the new go-to treatment for syphilis. However, the Tuskegee Experiment kept going. In 1941, many of the

MOVING ON FROM TUSKEGEE

In 2020 and 2021, lower Covid-19 vaccination figures for black Americans were linked back to the trauma and mistrust of Tuskegee. However, the descendants of the participants are actively working to break this cycle, with the group *Legacy of our Fathers* awarding young ancestors' scholarships to pursue degrees in bioethics and healthcare, and publicly speaking about informed medical care.

male patients joined the US military to fight in the Second World War. As part of military healthcare, every soldier was to be provided with syphilis treatment, but it was arranged for the 256 Tuskegee recruits to be given only a placebo. Yet the experiment could not be contained for much longer. As the 1940s progressed, the men had been receiving their supposed treatment for almost two decades but were only getting sicker. As they saw others receive penicillin and return to health, some began to secretly look for second opinions. By the early 1950s, almost 30 per cent of the participants had managed to get outside treatment, though only an estimated 7 per cent had enough adequate treatment before the programme management stepped in. The experiment's leaders were outraged, as it was only in the last few years that enough men had started dying for autopsies to be truly studied, with a third of the deaths caused by neurosyphilis and syphilitic complications. The deaths meant the experiment was working, with Wenger eagerly writing: '*We now know, where we could only surmise before, that we have contributed to their ailments and shortened their lives.*' If the patients received outside treatment now, the experiment would fail. So the programme leaders did the unthinkable and reached out to the doctors of the surrounding county, prohibiting them from treating the Tuskegee men. Through this action the patients were trapped, without medical care, and the experiment was able to continue until 1972.

That year, USPHS employee Peter Buxtun publicly exposed the Tuskegee Experiment. Buxtun had been filing official complaints over the ethics of the experiment since 1966, but had been constantly rebuffed. Seeing no other way to shut it down, in July 1972, he leaked the programme's information to the press. The public outcry forced the government's hand and in August the Tuskegee Syphilis Study Ad Hoc Advisory Panel was formed to investigate if the experiment could continue. It concluded that the study had *become* unethical, but put the onus of death on the patients themselves, stating that they may not have given informed consent for their lack of medical care, but that they had agreed to be part of the study, albeit based on false information. The Tuskegee Experiment was shut down, but by its end, only 74 of the participants were still alive – 28 men had died of syphilis, 100 more of related complications, and multiple partners of the men had unknowingly contracted syphilis, which in turn resulted in at least 19 children being born with congenital syphilis.

Yet the impact of the experiment wasn't isolated to this one ravaged community. In 2016, a study into the aftermath of the programme found that it had triggered a mass distrust of medical professionals and the Public Health Service, which in turn is estimated to have lowered the life expectancy of black American men by up to 1.5 years.

The Theatre of Theresienstadt

The machine that made the Holocaust work was one built around lies. Some of its first victims were those with mental and physical disabilities, who were targeted almost as soon as the Nazi Party came to power in 1933. What began as systematic sterilization had moved into mass execution by 1939, cloaked in secrecy and the spin word '*euthanasia*'. Starting with children with primarily developmental and learning disabilities, often parents were told their child was to receive specialized medical care, only to never see them again. False ashes and forged death certificates were sent home in the child's place. The success of these secret murders led the way for the inclusion of adults with similar disabilities and by 1940, specialized '*euthanasia*' centres and the use of gassing were in place. The foundation for the Final Solution had been set, but there was one major problem facing its creators. Though they had now killed at least 300,000 people, their plans for the Final Solution would involve millions. To keep the operation going, it would be imperative to contain these deaths, using censorship and secrecy at unprecedented levels. It was to this end that the ghetto of Theresienstadt was dreamed up: a middle point on the way to the death camps, a place for condemned Jews to wait to be transported to Auschwitz, but more importantly a puppet town that could be used to deceive international authorities, to prove that no matter what the rumours might have been, the Nazis were not killing Jewish people.

Built in 1780 by Holy Roman Emperor Joseph II, Theresienstadt was a small walled-off town in what is now the Czech Republic. It had been almost totally abandoned in the 1880s and by the 1930s only had a population of about 7,000. During the Nazi occupation of Czechoslovakia, the lands that encompassed Theresienstadt, Bohemia and Moravia were annexed, and in 1941, they were placed under the command of Reinhard Heydrich. Heydrich was one of the key architects in creating the Holocaust, and as part of his planning he had come up with the idea that to conceal the true nature of the extermination ahead, the Nazis needed a decoy. A model encampment which could be trotted out to promote the lie that under the Nazi regime, the Jewish people were being cared for. Theresienstadt was just the place, walled off and isolated, but with easy access to death camps. At the end of 1941, the residents of the town were evacuated and work on the new 'settlement' began.

Heydrich's initial vision for Theresienstadt was as a kind of faux retirement home. The official line on where Jewish people were being taken was to labour camps; however, suspicion was creeping in regarding elderly Jews – they couldn't undertake hard labour, so where were they going? To Theresienstadt. Heydrich gave the order for Jewish people over sixty-five, who had received medals in war, had been wounded or classed as war heroes, to be taken to the ghetto. To complete the ruse, these individuals were told they were to be rehomed, and were asked to sign away the rights to their properties and personal wealth in exchange for a '*lifelong guarantee of residential accommodations and board*' at Theresienstadt. In May 1942, a spanner was thrown in the works: Heydrich was assassinated, with his first 'model' prisoners due to arrive the next month. Rather than calling off the scheme, a replacement was quickly found in the shape of Adolf Eichmann – it was crucial that the façade to protect the Final Solution went ahead.

In June 1942, when the Jewish veterans arrived laden with furniture for their new homes, they realized they'd been duped. Instead, they were moved to cramped bunkhouses, whose beds were stacked up to the ceiling, leaving barely any room to move. Within weeks, malnutrition and disease were rife. Still, the next year, in June 1943, the first major attempt to use Theresienstadt for its proposed propaganda purpose took place, with two German Red Cross representatives invited for a tour. This failed beyond belief, with the representatives disgusted by what they saw and complaining of the overcrowded conditions. To combat this, in September, the decision was made to deport 5,000 people, mostly families, to Auschwitz. Instead of being immediately killed, the prisoners were set up in the newly created Theresienstadt family camp; their heads were not shaved; and they were allowed to wear civilian clothing. A requirement for the camp was that letters to the outside had to be written, describing the wonderful treatment that could be expected in Auschwitz, with the letters marked 'SB6' by guards – meaning the prisoner had preferential treatment, but would be killed in six months.

The failure of the 1943 Red Cross visit had made it clear that for Theresienstadt to work, it needed to become a kind of theatre. A pleasant-looking frontage, concealing the everyday horrors taking place behind the scenes. Its first performance would be crucial – convincing the Danish Red Cross that deportation of its Jewish people was humane. Since the first attempts to deport Denmark's Jews in September 1943, the Nazis had come across constant opposition. Civil servants, religious leaders, the Danish resistance and many members of the public did everything they could to leak information of raids, warn Jewish friends and family and assist in helping them flee or hide. On 1 October 1943, one scheduled round-up of Jews saw just 500 captured and 7,000 escaping. With the Danish Red Cross battering down their door to find out just *what* was going on at these camps, the Nazis decided the best thing to do was unveil the new Theresienstadt. At the end of 1943, a *'beautification'* programme commenced: 1,200 rose bushes were planted, a lush town square emerged, and shop façades were installed for everything from groceries to lingerie. A play park and bandstand were built, window boxes dotted tree-lined streets, and faux flats were given makeovers. By June 1944 it was ready.

The date for the Red Cross visit was fixed for 23 June. In the weeks before, those that were deemed to not fit the new aesthetic were sent to Auschwitz for liquidation, and the space they freed up was used to push forward the ghetto's elderly residents and promote the initial 'retirement community' lie. The remaining Jewish people were dressed in fashionable clothing and, under the constant eye of the SS, spent weeks practising their parts, whether that be watching children play in the park or 'shopping' in the town's centre. Finally, the day of the visit arrived, and over eight hours, the Red Cross were shown the Nazi-built fantasy. Apparently they were fooled, as in his final report, Dr Rossel, the representative from the Swiss arm of the Red Cross, happily noted: *'certainly there are few populations whose health is as carefully looked after as in Theresienstadt.'* For the Jews that had been forced to take part in this charade, realizing that the Red Cross would not intervene was crushing. According to Leo Baeck, a leader in Theresienstadt's council of elders: *'They appeared to be completely taken in by the false front put up for their benefit. ... Perhaps they knew the real conditions – but it looked as if they did not want to know the truth. The effect on our morale was devastating. We felt forgotten and forsaken.'*

Such was the success of the visit, it was decided a propaganda film should be made. The cast and director, the German actor and former co-star of Marlene Dietrich, Kurt Gerron, were plucked from the ghetto's prisoners and under SS supervision shooting began in the autumn of 1944. The title card read: *'The Führer gives Jews a city!'* and was followed by scenes of happy life in Theresienstadt, with peppy music playing as crowds cheered at a football game, cheery workers busied themselves on the factory floor, and women leaned against their front doors gossiping. Even dark rumours of gas chamber showers were eased, with a scene of men safely cleaning themselves in the communal shower. Once filming was over, Gerron and his cast were sent to Auschwitz and killed in the gas chambers. By the end of 1944, only an estimated 11,000 of Theresienstadt's inmates remained.

FINAL CUT

Gerron's ninety-minute film of Theresienstadt would never be released. The hope had been that it would sway international opinion and allow the Final Solution to be completed. But by the time its final cut was passed, it was March 1945, and the Nazis' defeat was looming. The film reel was destroyed, but twenty minutes survived in broken-up fragments. These can still be viewed today and provide a horrific window into perhaps one of the most perverse propaganda campaigns in history.

In March and April of 1945, two more visits by the Red Cross were made, and again, the representatives appeared to believe the lie placed in front of them. In late April, as the Allied forces began to liberate concentration camps, around 15,000 prisoners arrived at Theresienstadt, most survivors of death marches from other camps. With them came typhoid, which soon spread through the ghetto, killing roughly 1,500 people. Finally, on 2 May 1945, the Red Cross took over the camp's running, with the Soviet Union taking control in the coming days. An estimated 141,000 people, mostly Jewish, passed through Theresienstadt; of those, only 23,000 survived, the others dying in the ghetto or deported to death camps.

MAKING A TRAITOR: IVA TOGURI D'AQUINO

'Greetings everybody! This is your little playmate, I mean your bitter enemy, Ann, with a program of dangerous and wicked propaganda for my victims in the South Pacific.' This sarcastic 1944 Japanese broadcast to the American military would result in Iva Toguri D'Aquino being tried for treason and branded one of the worst US traitors in history. Ironically, Iva was born on Independence Day, 4 July 1916, to Japanese immigrant parents. She grew up in California, becoming a girl scout, a sorority sister, and a graduate in Zoology, before travelling to Japan in 1941 to look after her sick aunt. Within weeks of arriving, Iva was desperate to leave, as she barely spoke Japanese and was incredibly homesick. However, her plans were derailed when Japan attacked Pearl Harbor. Iva was now trapped, and after refusing to renounce her American citizenship, she was declared an enemy alien. In dire need of

a job, Iva ended up working as a typist for Japan's premier propaganda radio station – Radio Tokyo.

The idea of using overseas radio as both propaganda and psychological warfare came about a few months after Japan declared war on the Allies in December 1941. In May 1942, Japan and America agreed to exchange diplomats and interned people, and although this plan quickly fell apart, in August that year over 1,000 Japanese people arrived in Yokohama port from America to be repatriated. Hoping to increase Japanese propaganda output in America, many of the ship's passengers were questioned about where they got their news on Japan, with one of the most popular answers being the overseas radio station, Radio Tokyo. Immediately, work began to flood Radio Tokyo's airwaves with atrocity propaganda, which was soon joined by radio plays and monologues damning the American military. However, the Japanese Ambassador to Iran, Ichikawa Hikotaro, thought that they could be doing more. He'd noticed that many of the Allied forces listened to the radio output from the British Broadcasting Company (BBC), which interwove propaganda throughout its shows. However, unlike Radio Tokyo, the BBC played more than just propaganda, with music, interviews and likeable hosts drawing the soldiers in. Radio Tokyo turned about-face and began creating a block of programming aimed at Australian and American troops in and around Japan. The most prominent of these was *Zero Hour*, which was hosted by prisoners of war and played popular Western music. More crucially, the show included recordings of POWs reading letters to home and sharing news of their incarceration with their serving friends. If you wanted to hear how your captured friend was, then you had to listen to Radio Tokyo and its accompanying propaganda. This would have been an ingenious scheme, were it not for the fact the prisoners of war hosting *Zero Hour* were risking everything by turning it into an absolute farce.

The leader of *Zero Hour*'s team was Major Charles Cousens, who had previously worked as a radio producer in Sydney. He was joined by American Wallace Ince, and American-Filipino Norman Reyes, when it was then decided that *Zero Hour* needed a female host, so Iva Toguri D'Aquino was added to the mix. In November 1943, Iva debuted on the show, playing the role of '*Orphan Ann*', a Japanese woman who spread propaganda by spinning records. Iva would alter the script given to her by the propaganda team, insert patently ridiculous music choices, such as old accordion tracks and got around the censors by using American slang and talking quickly: '*Hello there, enemies! How's tricks? This is Ann of Radio Tokyo ... So be on your guard, and mind the children don't hear! All set? OK. Here's the first blow to your morale – the Boston Pops playing "Strike Up the Band!"*'

Iva's humour and constant sarcasm made her a favourite among the listening troops – however, she was struggling with her role at the station. In April 1944, Ince left the show after a beating from a guard left him unable to work, and he was followed by Cousens in June, who'd had a heart attack brought on from poor treatment in the prisoner-of-war camps. Without the team's leader, the higher-ups at Radio Tokyo took control of *Zero Hour*, with the team forced to drop their farce and focus on propaganda. In defiance, Iva stopped turning up for her shifts and Orphan Ann gradually disappeared from the airwaves.

PEARL HARBOR

On 7 December 1941, Japan carried out a surprise aerial attack on the US naval base Pearl Harbor in Hawaii. Along with the mass destruction of US planes and warships, 2,400 military personnel and civilians were killed. A day later, America would declare war on Japan.

In 1944, reports had started to emerge of the mysterious 'Tokyo Rose', the name US troops had given to Radio Tokyo's female propaganda presenter. This was likely initially Iva; however, in late 1944, when she'd stopped showing up at the station, she was replaced by multiple other women, including Miyeko Furuya and Ruth Hayakawa, who straightforwardly read the atrocity propaganda presented to them. In 1945, an investigation by the US Office of War Information concluded that there was no singular 'Tokyo Rose' but a collective of women: *'there is no Tokyo Rose; the name is strictly a GI invention.'* Still, following America's occupation of Japan in September 1945, a race began between journalists to unmask Tokyo Rose. *Cosmopolitan* reporter Harry Brundidge was tipped off that Iva had worked on *Zero Hour*, and he tracked her down. By this time, Iva was newly married to Portuguese-Japanese immigrant Filipe D'Aquino and the pair were desperately trying to buy their way back to America. Brundidge offered $2,000 for Iva to state that she was the original and only Tokyo Rose, a story they both knew not to be true. But, needing the money, Iva accepted. However, Brundidge's publisher refused to pay, and fearing that Iva might sue him, the journalist handed Iva's false confession to the Counterintelligence Corps. She was arrested and detained at Sugamo Prison in Yokohama for over a year before a lack of evidence caused the treason charges against her to be dropped.

During her detention, American newspapers had picked up the story of Tokyo Rose, and Iva was branded a traitor. In late 1946, she requested a new passport that would allow her to return to the US. Word of Iva's quest to come home reached gossip columnist Walter Winchell, who mounted a campaign to prevent her from entering the country, receiving support from J. Edgar Hoover and the Los Angeles City Council, which passed a resolution to prevent her from entering the county, where her parents now lived. As public venom intensified, President Truman's government was pressured to act – they'd been '*too soft on traitors*' and Tokyo Rose had to pay for her crimes. In September 1948, Iva was arrested again and deported to San Francisco, where she would be held ahead of trial. On 8 October, she was charged with eight counts of treason, and for almost a year she waited behind bars as the government prepared its case against her.

On 5 July 1949, the trial against Iva Toguri D'Aquino commenced. There was very little physical evidence, with many of the recordings of Iva's work on *Zero Hour* having been destroyed following her 1945 arrest. Of those that remained, none had any indication of treason, so the prosecution relied heavily on witness testimony, particularly that of Kenkichi Oki and George Mitsushio, two Japanese Americans who testified that Iva had broadcast herself celebrating an American ship's destruction. Major Charles Cousens flew in from Australia to defend Iva and explain the mocking tone of *Zero Hour*, but this fell on deaf ears. On 29 September, Iva was found guilty of one count of treason – using a microphone to spread information about the destruction of American ships. She was fined $10,000, stripped of her US citizenship, and sentenced to ten years in prison. However, she was paroled in 1956 and moved to live with her family in Chicago. Still, the label of traitor remained and Iva was constantly fending off threats and

attempts at deportation. Then, in 1976, everything changed – the *Chicago Tribune* published an investigation in which Oki and Mitsushio admitted to perjury, claiming they'd been threatened with treason trials of their own if they didn't lie in court. In 1977, Iva received a presidential pardon, clearing her name once and for all. To this day, she remains the only American ever pardoned for treason.

THE CENSUS DENIAL

In March 1942, while Iva Toguri D'Aquino was struggling to settle into her new life as an American alien in Japan, her parents were facing imprisonment in the US. In February, President Franklin D. Roosevelt signed Executive Order 9066, which cleared the path for Japanese people living in America to be confined to internment camps. Ostensibly, this was to prevent espionage and contain the '*Japanese threat*', despite the fact that a November 1941 report stated that there was no threat: '*the local Japanese are loyal to the United States or, at worst, hope that by remaining quiet they can avoid concentration camps or irresponsible mobs.*' Indeed, Assistant Secretary of War John McCloy would later recount that the decision to create the internment camps was primarily based around public perception, with animosity towards those of Japanese ancestry drastically increasing after the bombing of Pearl Harbor in December 1941. No matter why the decision was made, by

August 1942, over 100,000 of those living on America's West Coast were detained at makeshift camps, and by the end of the war, 120,000 people were living in Japanese internment camps, around 70,000 of whom were American citizens. But how was the internment so quickly rolled out? The answer is simple – the census.

In the 1930s, some use of census data began to take a dark turn, with several major incidences of the statistical data source being used to commit atrocities and violations of human rights on a vast scale. In 1936, the first Stalinist census was issued across the Soviet Union. This census was vital to provide the government with accurate data with which to create economic planning, but it would also reveal the mammoth number of deaths the regime had caused, particularly the millions that had died as a result of collectivized agriculture. As such, it was agreed that the census could never be publicly published; however, when the census data was completed in March 1937, the results shocked even Stalin. The sheer number of deaths was inescapable and the entire census was purged, the leading statisticians executed. When a census was published in 1939, it would be heavily doctored to reflect the strength of the regime. The other key misuse of census data was to locate minority groups. In 1938, the Netherlands began a campaign to improve its population registration system. This was to be a positive change, a way to follow its citizens from *cradle to grave* and improve the infrastructure around them. However, these great strides came to a startling halt when in 1941, a *'special registration'* system was created to locate and identify Jewish and Romani peoples. This was then used to detain and deport them to concentration and death camps. The strength of the Netherlands' population data system meant that although other countries, including Germany and Poland, used their census for the same reasons, the country's Jews would ultimately have one of the highest death rates of any occupied European country during the Holocaust.

THE CONCENTRATED TRUTH

Although publicly referred to as internment camps, the camps operated as concentration camps, with President Roosevelt himself referring to them as such. In 1946, Secretary of the Interior Harold Ickes would explain this internal use: 'We gave the fancy name of "relocation centers" to these dust bowls, but they were concentration camps nonetheless.'

Following the outbreak of the Second World War in September 1939, America's FBI and multiple military intelligence agencies requested access to census data pools of individuals, primarily to assess the number of citizens whose ancestry was linked to the Axis powers, Germany, Italy and Japan. However, William Lane Austin, the director of the US Census Bureau, denied access, as it went against the 1929 omnibus census statute, which stated that census data was for *'statistical purpose only'* and *'the Director of the Census* [could not] *permit anyone other than the sworn employees of the Census Office to examine the individual reports.'* As a result of his defiance, in 1940, Austin was forced to retire and, after a lengthy administrative back and forth, in March 1942, the Second War Powers Act became law. This entitled government agencies to have access to any data that was otherwise legally protected as confidential so long as it was *'for use in connection with the conduct of the war'*. Just like that, the 1940 census was free to be used in rounding up and interning America's Japanese citizens.

In the decades that followed the Second World War, multiple nations were transparent about the use of their statistical data in the detaining and deportation of minority groups, but America remained silent. However, in the late 1960s, a movement began within the Japanese American community seeking both acknowledgement and compensation for their treatment during the war. This became known as the Redress Movement, and as one of their pamphlets put it: *'redress for the injustices of 1942–1946 is not just an isolated Japanese American issue: it is an issue of concern for all Americans. Restitution does not put a price tag on freedom or justice. The issue is not to recover what cannot be recovered. The issue is to acknowledge the mistake by providing proper redress to victims of injustice, and thereby make such injustices less likely to recur.'*

During this period, pressure began to mount for the US Census Bureau to investigate its role in the internment. As activist and scholar Raymond Y. Okamura explained in a

1981 statement to the Commission on Wartime Relocation and Internment of Civilians: '*since the 1960 census, the Bureau has used the example of an alleged refusal to turn over names and addresses of Japanese Americans to the War Department in 1942 as their major selling point.*' Yet the Bureau claimed there was no evidence that it had ever released individual data in accordance with 1942's War Powers Act. In 1991, they slightly changed their tune, with long-time staffer Ed Goldfield claiming: '*As I understand it, what was finally worked out in the Japanese relocation and similar cases was that the Census Bureau provided what amounted to statistical information, but it did not identify individual Japanese.*'

This remained the party line until 2000, when two academics, Margo Anderson and William Seltzer, completed research deep-diving into the Bureau's archives, which found indisputable proof that the census had been used to roll out internment and abuse individual Japanese Americans' civil rights via the misuse of confidential information. For over sixty years, this had been not only denied, but used to gain trust. In 2000, an apology finally came, with Census Director Kenneth Prewitt acknowledging: '*the Census Bureau has described its role in such manner as to obfuscate its role in internment. Worst yet, some Census Bureau documents would lead the reader to believe that the Census Bureau behaved in a manner as to have actually protected the civil rights of Japanese Americans. This distortion of the historical record is being corrected.*'

OPERATION LEGACY

. . . .

In 2009, three elderly Kenyan men and two women sued the British government for atrocities committed against them by British colonial authorities during the Mau Mau Rebellion. Between 1952 and 1960, the Kenya Land and Freedom Army fought against British authority in Kenya. When the country had become a Crown colony in 1920, white settlers had pushed a lot of people out of their own land, particularly the Kikuyu, the largest ethnic group in Kenya. Now marginalized and without many political rights, they wanted their country back. In response, British colonial authorities unleashed their army, set up concentration camps, and began a routine of systematic brutality. The 2009 claimants said that under British orders they had experienced torture, sexual assault, and two of the men had been castrated. Yet despite the fact that Kenya had long since been removed from colonial rule, British authorities were incredibly evasive about looking into these claims. At first, they said there were no such files on the Mau Mau Rebellion. Then, in 2011, the government admitted that it had a stash of secret archives which included documents relating to the Mau Mau Rebellion, and finally the true reason for their evasive attitude was revealed – there had been evidence of the atrocities committed, but most of it was gone – the British government had burned it.

As the British Empire crumbled into the abyss in the twentieth century, from the 1940s onwards, several decades of decolonization programmes took place. Inherent to the handover of power was the passing on of governmental records, both past and present. Theoretically, Britain would hand over every document to incoming governments, but realistically, Britain didn't want to. To do that would mean handing newly independent nations evidence of every dark deed that had been committed against them during colonial rule. And so began a process of separating the so-called *'embarrassing'* records to be smuggled back to Britain. The problem was that sending so many documents back was incredibly time-consuming and most of the colonial offices lacked the manpower to do it with the secrecy it necessitated. So, a plan B quickly came into effect – send back what you can and just destroy the rest, or as one officer put it: *'What's burnt won't be missed.'*

To begin with, these burnings were ad hoc and often poorly thought out and executed. In 1947, over-eager officials at the Delhi colonial office burned so many records that a fog of smoke clung to the city for days. A slightly more organized effort was made in 1956 as British authorities prepared to remove themselves from Malaya. These records contained evidence of violence towards rebel groups, as well as mass deportations and arrests in ethnic Chinese communities, a massacre and burning of the village of Batang Kali, along with incidents of what was laughingly called *'jungle-bashing'*. The local colonial office decided what might be *'historically important'* and everything else was burned, this time using the British navy's incinerators in Singapore to avoid suspicion.

But what counted as historically important? This was a

question that created much hand-wringing for the staff in the Tanganyika (now Mainland Tanzania) colonial offices, who'd begun the process of destruction of records in December 1960. The process was overseen by Richard Clifford of the deputy governor's office in Dar es Salaam, who went to great strides in barring any African colleagues from viewing the records that were up for debate. The remaining staffers were told to skim the first few pages of historical documents and decide from that if they were to '*destroy the bulk of the paper*' or have it shipped back to Britain. The sheer volume of the archives and the frenzy to get through them all gave rise to the categorization of '*clean*' and '*dirty*' papers – if a paper had a whiff of anything bad, it was probably safest to put it on the pile for the bonfire. This methodology was then passed to the Ugandan offices, with Uganda also set on the path towards independence. However, the Ugandan office only had a small pool of white European workers, so if they were to get through all their records, they needed to bring in at least a few of their African colleagues. Britain's security service MI5 was firmly against this, and in a memo regarding one African-born assistant stressed that she couldn't work on the project as the terms under which she was first hired were '*different from now in that* [back then] *the handling of security papers was dealt with on a non-racial basis*'.

With the parameters of the racial bias set, the Ugandan offices soon included: '*all papers which might be interpreted as showing racial discrimination against Africans (or Negros in the USA)*' to the burn pile, along with anything that showed religious discrimination. By May 1961, in the wake of the Mau Mau Rebellion, the Kenyan colonial office began its document destruction process, picking up the methods that had been used in Uganda. Internal memos show the staffers panicking after an African colleague made a cup of tea for a clerical staffer working on the selection process. It was swiftly decided he *'should not be allowed to enter any of the offices during working hours'*. A further potential leak came when it was discovered that staff had taken to frantically hiding stacks of classified documents in the building, with a crate of records titled *'Psychological Warfare: Malaya'*, *'Kenya Colony Emergency Scheme'* and *'Intelligence and Security: Secret Reports'* found squirrelled away in a lift shaft. In a bid to quell this sea of hysteria and mistakes, in May 1961, Britain's Colonial Secretary, Iain Macleod, issued a telegram to the offices in Tanganyika, Uganda and Kenya, laying out official guidelines on selecting records and destroying them.

However, this proved relatively fruitless, as staff at the Kenyan offices weren't doing a great job of hiding the fact that they were *'re-organizing the archive'*, nor the accompanying fires they lit several times a week. In September 1961, British newspaper the *Guardian* reported on a *'Bonfire of Documents, Kenya Burning Secret Papers'*. To avoid any further exposure, far stricter instructions for the destruction of records were enforced, with the colonial office for Trinidad explaining in December 1961: *'We do not wish to celebrate Independence Day with a holocaust of burnt ODC* [Overseas Defence Committee] *papers.'* Instead, they opted to drown documents, weighing crates of records down and throwing them into the sea, preferably at night. Other offices began their processes of burning months in advance to prevent lingering clouds of smoke and ash, with Aden incinerating its records for over a year.

WHERE SECRETS LIE

The secret archive for those documents deemed worth saving was Hanslope Park, an MI6 and Foreign Office outstation in a sleepy patch of Buckinghamshire. It's estimated that the papers held took up a mile of shelving, with documents dating as far back as 1835. In 2013, the records were moved, and they are now held in the newly created Migrated Archive, in the National Archives.

What became known as Operation Legacy lasted well into the 1980s, maintaining its somewhat patchy veil of secrecy. In 2013, following the 2009 lawsuit, the British government announced the declassification of those files that had survived, with 19,957 files and documents finally becoming publicly available. Among these are *'destruction certificates'* sent by colonial offices to prove record destruction and note what had been destroyed. However, multiple internal memos from Operation Legacy show offices requesting permission to ignore this protocol, meaning that we will never know the full magnitude of exactly what was lost. In total, forty-one countries that we know of saw the mass destruction of their documented history during British decolonization. Britain may not have been able to rewrite its colonial history, but it certainly could burn it.

THE MIRABAL SISTERS COVER-UP

As dictators go, Rafael Trujillo was particularly bad. Since Trujillo had installed himself as the dictator of the Dominican Republic in August 1930, following a rigged presidential election marred by coercion and threats, his regime had quickly marked itself as one defined by an equal measure of terror and corruption. Two weeks after his inauguration, a hurricane swept through the Dominican Republic, killing thousands and destroying much of the country's infrastructure. Trujillo leapt upon this as an opportunity to gain control of the economy, using governmental decrees to seize banks' money, ringfence industry and declare states of emergency that would decrease workers' wages while diverting funds to his military. As his portfolio of industries bloomed, Trujillo used his presidential powers to shut down rival businesses and maintain a stranglehold of the market by issuing fixed governmental prices for everything from rice to cement. As for his opponents, Trujillo handled them with deadly force. It became a fixture of daily life for those who had publicly protested or questioned the rule of the president to disappear suddenly in the night.

Within a matter of years, Trujillo had gained total control of the Dominican Republic, from the government to the economy to his military. Banners and posters proclaimed '*Trujillo Forever!*' and '*We thank Trujillo for our water!*' The people were now living under a totalitarian regime, with Trujillo their Big Brother – he was everywhere and he was always watching. Growing up amidst this in the town of Ojo de Agua were the Mirabal sisters, Patria, Dedé, Minerva and María Teresa. The dictatorship was just part of their normality, like doing chores on the farm or going to school – they might not always like it, but it was ever-present. However, on 13 October 1949, Trujillo would shift from an obscure overseer to a very physical presence in the lives of the Mirabals. The dictator was hosting a party at his mansion in San Cristobal close to the sisters' home. He'd seen Minerva in a school play and selected her to be his new conquest, commanding the Mirabal family to attend his party, so he could woo the young woman. Yet, when Trujillo pulled Minerva for a dance, she rejected him. This had severe consequences for the sisters. Their father, Enrique, was imprisoned, while Minerva and her mother were held in a hotel for two months.

Even after her release, Trujillo didn't let go of his hold over Minerva. In 1952, she became a law student at the University of Santa Domingo; however, the president halted her second year of study until she attended a series of meetings with him. When she did graduate as one of the Dominican Republic's first female lawyers, Trujillo denied her right to practise law. Unable to work, Minerva married her fellow student Manuel Aurelio Tavárez Justo (known as Manolo) and settled down alongside her sisters for a quiet life as a wife and mother. At least she would on the surface.

THE PARSLEY MASSACRE

Alongside the everyday assassinations of Trujillo's regime were wholesale atrocities, notably, the Parsley Massacre in 1937, when on 2 October, the dictator ordered the execution of all Haitians living on the border between the Dominican Republic and Haiti, sparking a massacre that killed tens of thousands. Censorship around this was used to full effect, and those who later protested against the massacre disappeared.

In January 1960, Minerva and Manolo created an underground revolutionary group, the June 14th Movement. The name came from a failed uprising by the Dominican Liberation Movement in 1959, when a group of exiled Dominicans had tried to overthrow the Trujillo regime. Now, Minerva and her husband had taken the mantle, uniting dissidents in a series of localized cells. Patria and Maria Teresa joined the group and soon the sisters were sitting around their kitchen table making bombs and planning to take down a dictator.

Within days of the formal establishment of the group, Trujillo's forces moved in. On 20 January, Maria Teresa was arrested but released, then arrested again, this time alongside Minerva. The sisters were first detained in Trujillo's notorious *'special'* prison, LA 42, where torture and brutality had become systemized. A game of cat and mouse began. Maria Teresa and Minerva would be released and arrested, released and arrested again – as for the movement's other members, Trujillo was closing in, capturing, torturing and killing.

The June 14th Movement could not have sprung up at a worse time for the president. International opposition to his rule was starting to build, and in late January the Catholic Church denounced the regime in response to Trujillo's inhumane tactics against the movement. Yet no matter how many arrests were being made, the underground resistance kept on going. Then came another blow, when the Venezuelan president, Rómulo Betancourt, condemned the regime. In retaliation, in June, Trujillo orchestrated an assassination attempt against Betancourt, but this failed and Venezuela took its complaint to the Organization of American States. The Dominican Republic was sanctioned and America withdrew its support for the Trujillo regime. The president was now hanging on by a thread, and if the June 14th Movement carried on any longer, he could lose it all. The answer, Trujillo believed, was the Mirabal sisters, the maternal faces of the movement – if he got rid of them, the movement would fall in on itself.

A plan was made – Maria Teresa and Minerva's husbands were still imprisoned and on 25 November, they, along with Patria, were booked in to visit. The sisters' route to the prison included a stretch of road known for its high number of car accidents, and so it was arranged that they would be intercepted there. As the sisters drove home from the prison, their car was stopped and the women were forced to get into an unmarked vehicle, while their driver, Rufino de la Cruz, stayed in their Jeep. From there the Mirabal sisters were taken to a remote cane field, where they were strangled and their bodies beaten. Cruz had also been killed and the women's bloodied bodies were put back into the Jeep, which was duly pushed off the mountain road – a tragic traffic accident. The next day, reports of the deaths of Maria Teresa, Patria and Cruz were made public, Trujillo refusing to name Minerva.

Yet the cover-up was poorly executed, as the sisters had been snatched on a road in front of civilian witnesses. Despite Trujillo's censorship, the Dominican people saw through his story and understood that the faces of the resistance had been murdered in cold blood. This was the straw that broke the camel's back – a cornerstone of Trujillo's regime was the domestication of women, framing them as figures of maternal propriety to be looked after. Though he tortured and killed women in the opposition, this, like his sexual abuse, was censored. However, the Mirabal sisters' deaths could not be contained. The president had killed three women – three wives and mothers – undermining his own institution. By murdering the Mirabals, he hadn't broken the resistance, he'd just made it stronger. In the following months, dissent against the dictator snowballed, until finally, on 30 May 1961, Trujillo's own car was ambushed, and the president was shot and killed.

The following years would be a painful detachment from dictatorship, as the Dominican Republic slowly recovered. In 1962, the assassins who had killed the Mirabal sisters were put on trial – this would be the only trial relating to human rights violations committed during the Trujillo regime. The dictator may have been gone, but the fear around him hadn't and a veil of silence covered the country. However, one sister had survived, Dedé, the middle child. She'd not been involved in the movement, instead looking after the family and their farm. After her sisters' deaths, she'd not only taken on the care of their children but picked up the fight they'd been unable to carry through. Dedé used the public knowledge of her sisters' murders to help overcome the country's fear of censorship, utilizing their story to open up a dialogue around the atrocities committed under the Trujillo regime. For decades until her own death in 2014, Dedé worked tirelessly towards creating the democratic Dominican Republic and preserving the history of those who'd fallen in the name of freedom.

THE LEGACY OF LIES AT MỸ LAI

On 24 April 1968, the US Army completed an internal investigation into an attack which had predominately taken place in the small South Vietnamese hamlet of Mỹ Lai, one of four hamlets that made up the village of Son Mỹ. A month earlier, on 16 March, Charlie Company of the 11th Infantry Brigade, Americal Division, had been sent to take down the 48th Viet Cong Local Force Battalion, one of the deadliest arms of the Viet Cong, who'd been hiding out in Mỹ Lai. The army's investigation found that twenty civilians had died in the search and destroy operation; however, that number was far outweighed by the amount of Viet Cong deaths – the operation was nothing but a rousing success. Yet, in the army's barracks and camps, a far more disturbing version of events was being told.

On the morning of 16 March 1968, Charlie Company flanked Mỹ Lai on either side of the village. Led by Captain Ernest Medina on the ground, and with gunships flying overhead, the men were expecting a fight. Shortly before 7.30 a.m., they launched an artillery attack on the village to draw out the Viet Cong. However, Mỹ Lai remained silent. Flying above the scene running reconnaissance, Warrant Officer Hugh Thompson Jr radioed in a report that the Viet Cong were running away from the village – the fields and woods around Mỹ Lai were hot with Viet Cong, but the village itself was cold. On entering the village, that's exactly what the soldiers found – civilians, mainly the elderly, women and children, eating breakfast and starting their daily chores. But the company didn't move their efforts to the surrounding area; instead, they were ordered to carry out the initial plan – search and destroy.

WHAT ARE YOU FIGHTING FOR?

The Vietnam War began as a conflict between communist North Vietnam and South Vietnam, alongside its ally America, and would last from 1955 to 1975. Increasingly, tactics of guerrilla warfare were used, primarily by the Viet Cong, a southern Vietnamese arm of fighters aligned with the North.

Homes were razed to the ground as families hid inside. Officers ordered the villagers to be rounded up, taken into ditches and killed. One soldier shot himself in the foot so he could leave what was quickly becoming a massacre; however, most simply followed the orders they were given. At 8.30 a.m., confused helicopter units began radioing in sightings of what seemed to be piles of civilian bodies littering the roads towards Mỹ Lai. Nothing was done. Then, just before 10.30 a.m., Warrant Officer Thompson spotted Captain Medina following an injured woman into a field and shooting her twice at point-blank range. Thompson radioed in for the killing to stop, before landing and trying to intervene on the ground. There, he confronted Lieutenant William Calley Jr who was overseeing the mass execution of dozens of people. Calley claimed to be 'following orders'. Unable to stop the killing, Thompson instructed his own small unit to start evacuating as many people as possible. The massacre petered out at 11 a.m., when Captain Medina ordered that the men break for lunch. As the soldiers unpacked their meals in the smouldering ruins of Mỹ Lai, Thompson was back at the base making an official report on the massacre that had just unfolded. Rather than send out another unit to verify Thompson's claims, Captain Medina was asked to report civilian fatalities – he lied, recording only twenty to twenty-eight.

On 18 March, the soldiers of Charlie Company were instructed by Medina to keep quiet and not reveal what had happened. Once more, Thompson ignored this and continued to push his report, which was now joined by those from local Vietnamese authorities, one claiming that at least 400 civilians had been killed. The army begrudgingly agreed to an investigation but chose to barely use the reports of Thompson or the Vietnamese. Indeed, several of the Vietnamese reports that had been in the US Army's possession as late as 11 April were somehow lost by the time of the investigation's conclusion on the 24th of that month. Interestingly, many of the army's own reports that backed their findings of success at Mỹ Lai would also become 'lost' in the coming months.

This cover-up should have been the end of things. Though

the soldiers of Charlie Company were still telling their fellow soldiers of the massacre, these were stories that never went further than the mess hall. That was until Ronald Ridenhour got involved. A fellow member of the 11th Infantry Brigade, he'd trained alongside Charlie Company and it was through those friends that he'd heard what happened at Mỹ Lai. At first Ridenhour didn't believe them, putting it down to the wartime equivalent of a campfire story – a tall tale meant to shock, nothing more. But still, he somehow couldn't shake what he'd been told and in the months that followed, he started to ask around. Gradually, over the course of almost a year, Ridenhour compiled a stack of evidence revealing what had really happened at Mỹ Lai and on 29 March 1969, he put it all in a letter sent to Congress, the Department of Defense and President Nixon. For the most part, that letter was ignored, except for one recipient, Ridenhour's own congressman, Morris K. Udall, who forwarded the letter to the US Army and demanded a fresh investigation.

In late April 1969, a new investigation was launched, this time including the testimony and evidence of Charlie Company, with select GIs who were known to have actively participated in the killings, offered clemency in exchange for their full accounts. By September, enough evidence had been gathered to charge Calley with premeditated murder, with similar cases starting to be built against other key members of the company. Still, the US military was resolute in trying to keep a blanket of silence over Mỹ Lai. The scheme was ruined, however, on 13 November 1969, when freelance journalist Seymour

M. Hersh published an explosive article exposing Calley's murder charges. He quickly followed this with two articles containing charged interviews with Charlie Company soldiers in which they detailed the atrocities that had happened at Mỹ Lai. To further add to these revelations, Sergeant Ronald Haeberle, who'd been part of the Mỹ Lai operation, sold colour photographs that he'd secretly taken of the massacre to *Life* magazine. On 5 December, newsstands across America blared out Haeberle's pictures, which included devastating images of murdered babies and young children. The truth was out and no cover-up could put it back.

An in-depth investigation was launched, which officially granted credence to the atrocities that had happened. The Peers Investigation of 1970 found that at *'every command level from company to division, actions were taken or omitted which together effectively concealed from higher headquarters the events which transpired.'* Yet only one member of the company, Calley, was found guilty of murder. Of the twenty-six others who had been charged, all, including Captain Medina, were acquitted or had the charges dropped. On 29 March 1971, Calley was sentenced to life in prison, but he was set free in 1974. Following the investigation and trials, the Vietnam War Crimes Working Group was set up by the Pentagon as a task force to look into other potential military crimes. In 2003, journalist and historian Nick Turse discovered upon reading the since declassified documents that the task force had indeed substantiated numerous instances of war crimes, including seven other massacres; however, there were still 500 alleged war crimes that remained unsubstantiated, mostly due to lack of investigation.

And what of Mỹ Lai? There is no internationally agreed number of those who died that day; however, the most likely number of fatalities is the one given by the survivors – 504. Their names are inscribed on a golden wall in Mỹ Lai, much of which has since become both a museum and a memorial.

THE CHERNOBYL DISASTER

On the night of 25–26 April 1986, the Chernobyl nuclear power plant in Ukraine saw an explosion in its fourth unit. This was just the latest in a long line of accidents at nuclear plants within the Soviet Union, yet it would be the most catastrophic, its blast creating cataclysmic ramifications that are expected to last for tens of thousands of years.

The run-up to and the aftermath of Chernobyl were steeped in lies and omission. At the time of the disaster, the Soviet Union was one of the global leaders in nuclear power production and had committed itself to a future built upon the energy source. Yet despite this, it had one of the poorest safety regulations systems within the sector. Cost-cutting was paramount. Ukrainian journalist Lyubov Kovalevskaya was a reporter and editor for Chernobyl's local paper and recalled that as the plant was being built it suffered constant issues with low staffing, incompatible materials and equipment shortages, beginning a cycle of sub-par construction and safety: '*The problems of the first energy block were passed on to the second, from the second to the third, and so on.*' Corners were cut even in designing the plant's high-power channel-type reactor (RBMK), making accidents not something to be avoided, but inevitabilities. Yet this was just part of the Soviet Union's nuclear structure – accidents would happen, but intentional design flaws should only create relatively minor accidents – everything would probably be fine. This is not a stance commonly associated with nuclear infrastructure, but for the most part, the Soviet plan to ignore and hope for the best worked out. Prior to 1986, there had been a series of accidents, including one in 1975 at the Leningrad Nuclear Power Plant and another in 1982 at Chernobyl, both of which had resulted in radiation leaking throughout the plant and the nearby environment, but whose reactors were saved and soon returned to working order. A month before the disastrous accident at Chernobyl, Kovalevskaya would actually publish an exposé revealing the numerous safety issues that were being covered up at the plant, yet her article, ironically titled '*Not so private an issue*', would be shrugged off as lies by the nuclear power officials.

Nuclear power was tantamount to the success of the USSR. When the Iron Curtain was drawn, the Soviet Union was quick to release propaganda explaining how its citizens would survive any Cold War nuclear strike. To hold on to power, they needed to show their people and the international world at large that they had a grip on nuclear arms and technology, and so it was better to hide any accidents than admit to them. This stance was demonstrated in 1957, when the Soviet Union was racing to catch up with America in nuclear weapons research and production. In September that year, there was an accident at a top-secret plutonium production site in Mayak. Like Chernobyl, this site had been built fast and cheaply, with safety regulations falling by the wayside, and as such nuclear waste was not properly disposed of, leading to a chemical explosion in September 1957 that released huge amounts of radioactivity into the atmosphere and exposed an estimated 500,000 people to high levels of radiation. Yet the Soviet government chose not to report the accident publicly, putting off evacuations for a week and, even then, only evacuating 11,000 people who were given false reasons for their removal. The explosion itself was rebranded as an experimental large-scale release – there was no danger. Of course, there *was* danger; the extreme radiation levels caused a myriad of health conditions, particularly cancer.

Despite the high death toll in the coming decades, the Mayak disaster was so well covered up that it wouldn't be until the fall of the USSR in 1991 that it became public knowledge. So it made sense that in the 1970s, when Soviet civil defence began planning for the aftermath of a major nuclear accident, they drew from the lessons learned at Mayak. Public health was not the priority, it was protecting the reputation of the Soviet Union – lie and cover-up. Prior to the Chernobyl explosion, the USSR did not officially recognize any major nuclear accidents, despite there being a litany of them. It was hoped that Chernobyl would be the same. Indeed, it wasn't the Soviet Union that first informed neighbouring countries of the high levels of radiation blasted towards them in the early hours of 26 April 1986, but the team at Swedish power plant Forsmark. Their findings came two days after the disaster unfolded, on 28 April. A sensor detected startling levels of radiation on a Forsmark worker's shoes, and an investigation began. Following the discovery that the leak wasn't coming from the plant itself, the grass the worker had just walked across was analysed and radioactive particles specific to Soviet plants were found. Their backs to the wall, the USSR had to admit to the disaster.

COST OF THE SPACE RACE

A large reason for the secrecy around the disaster in Mayak was that it happened just days before the Soviet Union was due to launch Sputnik 1 on 4 October 1957. This was to be the first artificial Earth satellite and a monumental blow to the US in the space race. Admitting to a catastrophic nuclear accident didn't play into the propaganda tale and so it was covered up.

As the world was just waking up to the news of Chernobyl, many of those living in the radiation-saturated area were still there. The city of Pripyat had begun evacuating its citizens on the afternoon of 27 April, though none were told why or given any advice on how to protect themselves from the radiation. The reason for this was, once more, secrecy. Discussion of evacuations had begun almost as soon as the disaster occurred; in a 6 a.m. meeting on 26 April, plant and government officials debated the urgency, in the knowledge that firefighters at the plant were already dying of radiation sickness just hours after coming into contact with Chernobyl. Though members of the Civil Defense and Ministry of Internal Affairs pushed for immediate evacuation, the need for a veil of secrecy that the Soviet Union had cemented in officials' minds won out. Pripyat was begrudgingly evacuated, but those living in smaller towns and cities within Chernobyl's district remained totally oblivious to the danger they were in. Aware that more people would die if they stalled, the GO continued to press for action in the coming days, but readying nearby citizens for evacuation through a radio broadcast would only negate the cover-up already in progress. Luckily, on 29 April, the international press began hurriedly reporting on the disaster – the USSR needed to at least act as if they'd been doing more than crossing their fingers and hoping it would all go away.

In the coming days, slowly but surely, more evacuations took place. Still, the Soviet Union wouldn't admit to how disastrous the explosion had been and, as such, any attempts to get people out of the danger zones were hampered by governmental red tape. This was combined with a failure to properly distribute potassium iodide to those affected – though the USSR had stockpiles ready, to give them out would be to show that the international press was right, and the Soviet Union had overseen a totally avoidable nuclear catastrophe. So many were left without treatment and, in turn, developed internal radiation exposure. Though the government hadn't been able to fully cover up the extent of the damage, as they had at Mayak, they had once more considered the health of their people as secondary to the establishment's reputation.

In the days and weeks that followed the international outing of the explosion, the Soviet Union released its own cloud of lies in an attempt to mitigate the real damage. As journalists like Lyubov Kovalevskaya risked their lives by entering the radiation zones, their efforts to release the truth were dogged by KGB agents. Indeed, it wouldn't be until after the USSR fell that the full extent of Chernobyl's ravages and the lies to conceal them started to unspool. We'll never know exactly how many deaths Chernobyl will have caused, but according to the Clinical Institute of Radiation Medicine and Endocrinology in Minsk, Belarus, there was a 40 per cent uptick in cancer diagnosis between 1990 and 2000. As for the environmental damage, the areas immediately around Chernobyl are unlikely to be habitable for another 20,000 years.

AFTERWORD

So much of what we know about history is entrenched in lies and omissions. Much like the bumbling bureaucrats of Operation Legacy, the moments in history we universally deem to be worth remembering are often picked without much thought. We want a good story, a hero and a villain, to feel good about ourselves and our country. We don't like to be asked too much, to dwell on the unthinkable aspects of our pasts. That's understandable; after all, as we've seen, it's how history consumption has worked for centuries. Indeed, it's a fate that befell many of the moments covered in this book. But that doesn't mean it's healthy and it's certainly not sustainable.

Following the Second World War, there was a sudden growth in the academic study of memory, particularly how we understand and remember atrocities. From this, we've learned and are still learning a lot, for example, the importance of public memorials, museums and the intertwining of education in maintaining and understanding these moments in history. There's another lesson that on reflection is fairly obvious – when we ignore, disavow or push away these moments, it's inherently detrimental. In the immediate, this creates a divide between countries and people. Political and psychological rifts that are hard to recover from. The longer this festers, the worse the fracture becomes, often transforming into conspiracy theories and further lies that pour so much misinformation onto the already boggy world of historical understanding.

Although we're taught in school that history should be unbiased, it inescapably isn't. But that doesn't mean that we as history readers need to be biased ourselves. Nobody likes not having the whole story – you don't buy a novel and rip out the middle, so why do the same with history? I hope you leave this book wanting to know more, and I know that you'll enjoy finding those answers.

ACKNOWLEDGEMENTS

Thank you to my wonderful husband Simon; this book would not have been possible without your constant support and cups of coffee! To my mum and sister, Becky, as well as my gorgeous nephew, Harrison, who fill every day with laughter and love. A huge thanks to my agent Donald Winchester for taking a chance and to the entire team at Michael O'Mara Books, particularly Louise Dixon and Gabriella Nemeth for your expertise and patience.

SELECT BIBLIOGRAPHY

Bergin, Joseph, Broedel, Hans, Roberts, Penny, Naphy, William G., *The 'Malleus Maleficarum' and the Construction of Witchcraft: Theology and Popular Belief* (Manchester University Press, 2004)

Brand, Charles M., *Byzantium Confronts the West, 1180–1204* (Harvard University Press, 1964)

Cobain, Ian, *The History Thieves: Secrets, Lies and the Shaping of a Modern Nation* (Portobello Books, 2016)

Dalrymple, William, *The Anarchy – The Relentless Rise of the East India Company* (Bloomsbury Publishing, 2020)

Dwyer, Philip, Ryan, Lyndall, *Theatres of Violence: Massacre, Mass Killing and Atrocity Throughout History* (Berghahn Books, 2012)

Harvey, Karen, *The Imposteress Rabbit Breeder: Mary Toft and Eighteenth-Century England* (OUP Oxford, 2020)

Hayashi, Brian Masaru, *Democratizing the Enemy: The Japanese American Internment* (Princeton University Press, 2008)

Hunt, Lynn, *Eroticism and the Body Politic* (Johns Hopkins University Press, 1991)

Restall, Matthew, *Seven Myths of the Spanish Conquest* (Oxford University Press, 2004)

Smith, Mark B., *The Russia Anxiety: And How History Can Resolve It* (Allen Lane, 2019)

Sodaro, Amy, *Exhibiting Atrocity: Memorial Museums and the Politics of Past Violence* (Knowledge Unlatched, 2017)

Teter, Magda, *Blood Libel: On the Trail of an Antisemitic Myth* (Harvard University Press, 2020)

Townsend, Camilla, *Fifth Sun: A New History of the Aztecs* (Oxford University Press, 2019)

INDEX